A HEALING
YEAR

A HEALING YEAR

DAILY MEDITATIONS
FOR LIVING WITH LOSS

Alaric Lewis

PUBLICATIONS

A HEALING YEAR
Daily Meditations for Living with Loss
by Alaric Lewis

Edited by L. C. Fiore
Cover design by Tom A. Wright
Cover art by Kathryn Schnabel
Text design and typesetting by Patricia A. Lynch

Scripture quotations are from the *New Revised Standard Version Bible*, copyright
© 1989 by the Division of Christian Education of the National Council of the
Churches of Christ in the USA. Used by permission.

Text © 2000, 2007 by Alaric Lewis

Published by ACTA PUBLICATIONS, 5559 W. Howard St., Skokie, IL
800-397-2282, www.actapublications.com

Library of Congress Catalog Number: 2007926288

ISBN: 978-0-8-7946-337-3

Printed in the United States of America by Evangel Press
Year: 12 11 10 09 08 07
Printing: 10 9 8 7 6 5 4 3 2 1

This book is dedicated
to the memory of
my mother, Shirley Jean Lewis.

My mother died when I was seven years old. At a time when most children were concerned with nothing more than their play, I was facing questions that I would rather not have faced: What happens when people die? Will I ever feel happy again? What can I do for my family to help them with all of this? Did I do something to bring this about? Why, God, why?

My grandmother died when I was twenty-two. Surely now the questions would be easier to face, I thought. But they were not. Because not only did I have to deal with loss all over again, this loss touched something within me that was still very connected to the loss of my mother, which was connected to other losses, which were somehow connected to God.

My grandfather died when I was twenty-eight. I was, at this point, a priest serving in an active parish, and had been with countless families, offering comfort and solace to those who mourned. Surely I would have more answers this time, I thought. Again, this loss was connected to the losses of my mother and grandmother, which were connected to other losses, which were somehow connected to God.

They're all very complicated, these issues of grief and loss which we must face. Just when we think we have moved on to a new place, something will come up within us that touches it all off again. And, though we thought that all our tears had been shed, though we thought that the aching in our hearts had vanished, the tears and the ache can and do return. And with them come the questions: What happens when people die? Will I ever feel happy again? What can I do for my family to help them with all of this? Did I do something to bring this about? Why, God, why?

Although I don't purport to know all the answers, I have begun to discern a very fundamental truth weaving through it all: The best way to understand loss and the grief that comes from it, the best way to begin to comprehend the toll that death can take on the living, is to be aware of the presence of God in our daily lives. If we look for answers elsewhere, our pursuits are worthless.

This book, then, offers reflections for each day of the year. It is my attempt to point out the amazing presence of God in this world and to offer—if not the answers—at least my attempts to search for them. Some of the experiences I relate are unique to me, but the truths these experiences relate are as common as humankind. I am absolutely convinced that God is active in our lives in so many ways, and that if we begin to listen for His presence, to see Him in others, to feel Him in our hearts, then the sheer suffering and pain of loss can be transformed in our hearts. With God's abundant help, we can begin to truly heal: one day at a time.

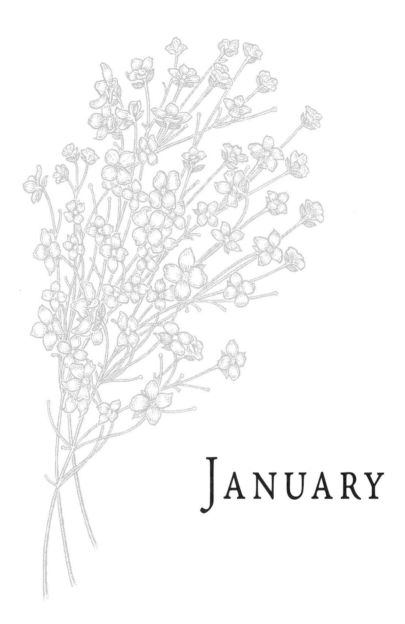

JANUARY

❦ 1 ❦

Begin at the beginning...and go on till you come
to the end: then stop.

LEWIS CARROLL

I resolve to quit smoking. I resolve to lose weight. I resolve to exercise more. I resolve to eat right. I resolve to relax more. Each year we draw up our list of New Year's resolutions as if the fact that another calendar year has begun is going to make sure we are spurred onto action, into growth. And often the list can be laid aside or even forgotten.

There is nothing magical about the first day of January however, and it is important for us to realize that life itself is a series of unending patterns of beginnings and endings, beginnings and endings. And somewhere, in between all of these beginnings and endings, we live. And in living we find grace. And in finding grace we find the courage and strength to begin again.

❦ 2 ❦

Little children, let us love not in word or speech,
but in truth and action.

1 JOHN 3:18

There comes a time when we have to put our money where our mouth is. There comes a time when we move from *talking* about love—what it means, how it touches us, how wonderful it is—to *doing* something to make love more present, more real. And harsh as it may sound, if we expect others to show us love, to help us through rough times, then we need to show that same love to others, even when we feel there is very little we can give or very little we can do. How will the people in our lives know how to love us—to show us love—if we do not show them?

❧ 3 ❧

Keep thou my feet: I do not ask to see
The distant scene; one step enough for me.

JOHN HENRY CARDINAL NEWMAN

If only we could see the future, we might think, how much easier life would be. When we wonder how we are going to get through something, it would be a comfort to know just how we will get through it—and when. When we wonder if things will ever be better, it would be nice to know that they will.

Of course, we cannot know. Only God knows. And God doesn't ordinarily let us know what will happen in the future. But He does promise to guide our steps. If we concentrate on those steps, and where they are leading us now, then we can be sure that we will not be led into anything that is beyond our ability to handle.

❧ 4 ❧

Do what you can, with what you have, where you are.

THEODORE ROOSEVELT

My sister Kathy and I, extroverts, like to talk about our mother as much as we can. We want to talk about everything—what she was like, whether she could sing, how she struggled when she was in pain, what really made her angry, what music she liked—everything. My brother David, more of an introvert, seems to prefer to keep his memories in his own heart where he can deal with them in his own way. To expect my sister or me to pipe down, or my brother to start launching into soliloquies, is to turn a blind eye to the fact that we all need to work through not just grief but life itself, with the personality and quirks and interesting attributes we've been given.

❧ 5 ❧

The saying is sure:
If we have died with him, we will also live with him;
If we endure, we will also reign with him.

2 TIMOTHY 2:11-12

If only dying with Him and holding out to the end was easier, this business of reigning with Him might appear more attractive than it does at first glance. But we know death—either the dying to self that Christians undergo or the real physical death that our loved ones experience—is far from easy. It makes stringent demands on us, causes us to suffer and to question. And what about "holding out," or endurance? How difficult it is to endure, when at our lowest times it all can seem like folly...like waste.

❧ 6 ❧

Of all the things that wisdom provides to make life entirely happy,
much the greatest is the possession of friendship.

EPICURUS

The phone call came, telling me of my grandfather's death. I slumped by the side of the bed, anguished and frightened. I did not want to—indeed I could not—imagine a world in which Gramps didn't tell me stories and fix things for me and make me feel part of his life. I immediately reached for that same phone and called my friend Godfrey, because I knew that things could look different in the light of friendship. And I made a resolution to never block out that light from my life.

7

The art of living is more like wrestling than dancing.
MARCUS AURELIUS

When we are young we think that life should be one joy after another and that we should glide through it blissfully, turning and twirling with delight at the sheer wonder and adventure of it all. As we grow older, cynicism takes over, and we might think of life more in terms of a battle with constant skirmishes that require our utmost strength and daily attention.

It seems to me the healthiest stance is somewhere in between. Because there are indeed battles in life that can drain us of our energy and wound us. But once the battle is over, perhaps the best thing to do is cast off our armor and dance for joy that the battle didn't kill us—and that it was somehow worth the fight.

8

There is nothing so strong as gentleness,
and nothing so gentle as real strength.
SAINT FRANCIS DE SALES

Once when I was a very young boy, my Gramps gave into my whining and agreed to let me hammer a nail into a board he was working on. Wanting to impress him with the sheer power of my six-year-old muscles, I swung the hammer with all my might: and missed the nail. I swung again and again. And I missed again and again. Gramps finally took the hammer out of my hand and tapped the nail securely in place. An important lesson for a young boy to learn: Sometimes the small, quiet way of dealing with a situation is exactly the way to ensure something gets done.

❦9❦

You cause the grass to grow for the cattle
and the plants for people to use.

Psalm 104

When I was a young boy, I was fascinated by gardens. A garden was a magical, wondrous place. After my mother died, nothing in my world seemed to be normal or uniform except gardens that offered their testimony to order in the world. Seeds were laid precisely in a row; each thing had its place where loving hands tucked the seeds into a bed of the earth, just like a mother. And as I saw new life make its way to the top of the soil, I thought how amazing that something as frail as a plant could have the strength to push aside so much soil. How wondrous it was when the plants grew to full size. I could stand among the corn and be completely hidden from the world whenever it began to confuse me.

*How amazing that something
as frail as a plant
could have the strength
to push aside so much soil.*

❧ 10 ❧

Very truly, I tell you, unless a grain of wheat falls into the earth and dies, it remains just a single grain; but if it dies, it bears much fruit.

JOHN 12:24

I never saw what happened to the seed. I never reflected on the dark, cold indifference of the earth. It never dawned on me that the hard exterior of the shell had to crack open and give way to the life inside. Mesmerized by this new life, I hid myself in the shelter of full-grown plants, never considering at what cost this growth occurred. Perhaps if as a small child I had known the violent reality of the seed, then the garden wouldn't have seemed so wondrous, so magical. I know now of course that it is precisely *because* of the violent reality of the seed that the plant emerges triumphant and beautiful. It is not in spite of the traumas of the dark, cold soil that beauty emerges, but because of it.

❧ 11 ❧

Human excellence means nothing
unless it works with the consent of God.

EURIPIDES

Fire; the wheel; iron tools; the printing press; the steam engine; the telephone; the computer. The history of the human race is marked with amazing accomplishments. When we put our minds to it, we are quite resourceful. The problem comes when we expect to invent and fix ourselves as easily as we invent and fix objects—we just can't. We need to realize God is the true inventor, and if we have difficulty getting through things in this life we have to be content that God is the one who will make things new in us—but on His time, not necessarily on ours. It is a little lesson in humilty when we are forced to recognize we are not always the creator, but rather a work ourselves, still very much in progress.

❧ 12 ❧

Call on me in the day of trouble.

PSALM 50

People say they don't want to ask God for something because it seems the only time they turn to Him is when they need something. They don't want to be hypocritical—needing Him when times are bad but not when times are good. Prayers of thanksgiving should be part of our life, but if we forget on occasion to tell God thanks it does not mean we shouldn't continue to cry out to Him in our need. The Lord longs to be a part of our lives, however that may manifest itself. He longs to comfort us in our sorrows, soothe our pain, be with us so we are never alone. Let us never hesitate to call on Him for any reason. For if we do cry out to Him in distress, we might have something to thank Him for...soon.

❧ 13 ❧

The cause of Freedom is the cause of God!

EPICURUS

The people of Israel were in bondage. Deprived of liberty, shackled to the harsh realities of a life beyond their control, they cried out to their God, "Deliver us!" And God sent them Moses, a man also born of slaves. God heard their cry and wanted His people to know blessed freedom. And they did.

To us God sent His Son, born of a woman, because God heard our cry. He wanted us to know blessed freedom. And now we do.

When we find ourselves imprisoned, we must realize that God desires us to be free. And so we must cry out to Him, and He will set us free.

❦ 14 ❦

Clergymen and people who use phrases without wisdom sometimes talk of suffering as a mystery. It is really a revelation.

OSCAR WILDE

"Why?" I cried in sorrow as a young boy, confused by a world where children could be motherless. "Why?" I still cry as a young man, confused by a world where senseless brutality seems to surround me at times. And the world spins silently on its perch, and no answer is given me except the answer of the Cross, in the shadow of which the world is cast. It is the answer to all of our exasperated questions. In its silence we learn not only about the world, but about our very souls.

❦ 15 ❦

Everything you can imagine is real.

PABLO PICASSO

Picasso's genius stemmed from seeing the world and its inhabitants in ways that no one else ever had. He imagined a world where the soft ambiguity of the human form and the soft impressions of nature were transformed into stern geometric shapes and vibrant colors, inviting his viewers to reflect on the wonders of humanity and of the world in new ways. Such was the amazing power of his imagination.

Human beings by nature are imaginative people, and we rely on our imagination. It is good for us to imagine a world of selfless beauty and love. If we live with the struggles and sadness of loss, we need to imagine a time when the pain will be lessened, the sadness not as gripping. Then we can begin to make the transition from a life imagined to a life lived.

❧ 16 ❧

Such is the confidence that we have through Christ, toward God.

2 CORINTHIANS 3:4

Many people constantly search for more confidence. We need only turn on our television sets late at night to see a toothy man telling us how we can take charge of our lives and be confident in our abilities, our business transactions, and our relationships. All of this for three easy installments of $49.99.

I think all of the people who offer their versions of confidence miss the boat. We must first and foremost work on our faith life, have confidence in God's mercy, His redeeming love, His place in our lives and in the lives of others. If we can be confident of these things, then we may begin to view our abilities, our business transactions, our relationships—our very lives—with the confidence that can only come from Christ.

❧ 17 ❧

I took them up in my arms,
but they did not know that I healed them.

HOSEA 11:3

Most of us know what it means to be healed in one fashion or another. For some of us it is the relief of getting over a cold that we thought would never go away. For some of us it is the blessed relief of a successful surgery and recovery. For some of us it is the peace of mind of being forgiven. Whatever the case, we are nourished by moments of healing; like mother's milk these moments strengthen us and allow us to grow.

It does us good to recognize that every moment of healing in our lives is of God, who like a mother loves us and stoops down to offer us nourishment. If we are in need of healing of any kind, let us never fail to reach for Him.

❦ 18 ❦

Great thoughts come from the heart.
MARQUIS DE VAUVENARGUES

A few years ago I was looking out the window of my office and I saw a mother walking her third-grade son to the school corner, sending him off with a hug. I was suddenly overcome with sadness, acutely aware of my own third-grade year in which no mother was there to fulfill this important task. How ridiculous, I thought at first: I am an adult, and it was years ago. It doesn't make sense that I should be so affected so many years later. But then I realized that I was thinking with my mind, a mind that says everything should be fine now. Instead I needed to think with my heart, a heart that said that moment of sadness—although I didn't understand it then—was a gift.

❦ 19 ❦

Life seems to me like a Japanese picture
which our imagination does not allow to end in the margin.
OLIVER WENDELL HOLMES, JR.

Most of us are raised on the notion of Heaven, that people go to a place of beauty and serenity when they die. And the reality of Heaven is a wonderful thing: It helps soothe the pain of loss and offers hope to us who still toil on the earth.

Whereas John Lennon encouraged people to "imagine there's no Heaven," I would encourage just the opposite. The mysteries of life and love cannot be limited to time and space, and if the beautiful colors of our memories of loved ones—and their memories of us—somehow spill out over the margins of our finite lives, so be it. It gives us a glimpse here on earth of the beautiful portrait of eternity.

❧ 20 ❧

He said to me, "Mortal, can these bones live?"

EZEKIEL 37:3

How amazing: bare bones slowly developing sinews; flesh appearing; and then, emboldened by the very breath of God the bones spring to life, dancing the ecstatic jig of those given life by God. Where once there was nothing but dust and death, with God life springs forth. How amazing.

He seeks to come to us as well. Our own bones, made stiff from sorrow, dried up from grief, can be given new life if we but allow that same breath to blow over us and through us. We must desire to change and to grow closer to the one who calls our tired bones to dance. But if we can receive the grace to change, what an amazing dance it can be: one that can carry us all the way to eternity.

❧ 21 ❧

From the rising of the sun to its setting
the name of the Lord is to be praised.

PSALM 113

In the midst of one of those bad/sad/angry/bewildered moods that can strike us all at any time, I was walking through our living room at about 6:30 in the morning. The autumn sun was just beginning to rise over the valley below and breathtaking colors began to appear over the misty horizon. I stopped and marveled at the mastery of it all, and realized that the Painter was doing it all for me, wanting me to share in the beauty. That a million other eyes could behold a sunrise didn't seem to matter; at that moment, in that place, it was clearly done just for me.

❧ 22 ❧

Yesternight the sun went hence,
And yet is here today.

JOHN DONNE

The next morning, after darkness had once again reclaimed the earth, I went to stand at my east-facing window, needing to experience once again the blessed promise that the sun's rays seem to be able to paint upon my soul. And standing there, also receiving my sun, was Brother Robert, staring at the portrait unfolding before him. How dare him, I thought at first. That sun was made for me. But then a calm came over me as I realized that, just as I had needed to be healed by beauty, perhaps he too needed the same thing. And God provided for him as He did for me.

❧ 23 ❧

And after the earthquake a fire,
but the Lord was not in the fire:
And after the fire a sound of sheer silence.

1 KINGS 19:12

What an awe-inspiring and frightening prospect Elijah faced. "Go to the mouth of the cave," God told him, "and I will pass by." The wind roared, rocks were crushed, the earth quaked and the air around him burst into flames—much of the theatrics one would expect from an all-powerful God. And yet, God was in none of that. "No," He seemed to be saying to Elijah, "if you want to feel My presence, if you want to know that I am here with you, look not to dramatics and sound effects, listen to the small whispering voice within you."

He says the same to us. And we realize that if God can enter into the quiet secret place of our hearts, then He most certainly can touch anything that is already there. What an awe-inspiring and frightening prospect.

❧24❧

Thus happiness depends, as Nature shows,
Less on exterior things than most suppose.

WILLIAM COWPER

"If only I would win the lottery," people say and then go on to list the things they would procure that would make their lives better. Swimming pools, cars, better homes, vacations—all of these things would so crowd life with new-found happiness that there would be little room for anything else, much less sorrow.

It's hard to convince people that the true key to happiness lies in a heart open to what the Lord desires. And that the Lord may desire for us things other than possessions is a fact quite often ignored.

❧25❧

Under his wings you will find refuge.

PSALM 91

"He always put this umbrella up for me when the sun got too bad," a recently-widowed woman lamented to me one day when I was sitting with her on her patio. Her shaky hands shielded her eyes from the afternoon glare. I jumped up and did just that, realizing as I did that she wasn't simply lamenting the sun in her eyes but a sense of security, of being taken care of. Death had stripped her of these things. And so I started telling stories of our God who cared so passionately for us, who longed to shelter us in the wings of love. And in very different words she told me stories of the same love and care, as the sun crept below the grain elevator on the horizon.

❧26❧

W here there is sorrow there is holy ground.

OSCAR WILDE

Perhaps the most jarring part of a monastic funeral is at the cemetery, when the abbot throws a shovel full of dirt on the coffin already placed in the earth. Visitors inevitably jump as the sound echoes through the pine trees, as if an earthquake has disturbed the peacefulness of the gathering. Thud: It is the sound of hearts breaking. Thud: It is the sound of voiceless crying. Thud: It is the sound of pain, of loss.

It is undeniable, however, that it is also the sound of something sacred, for that thud is a testimony not only to the reality and finality of loss but also to the reality and finality of God's love, manifested by the image of a cross standing against the blood-red sky while the earth quaked in reverence.

❧27❧

L et me sing for my beloved
my love song concerning his vineyard.

ISAIAH 5:1

In the afternoon haze of the courts of Jerusalem, they heard his voice. Who was this prophet, this Isaiah, who spoke to them? Intrigued, they gathered closer to listen. He spoke to them of a beautiful vineyard on a hillside, and with the power of his words painted pictures in their minds so intense and detailed that the finest of painters could not begin to capture them. And so they listened, transfixed on the brush strokes that were his words and images. But then something happened. In the midst of his amazing words, the picture suddenly became too clear. These wild grapes were the listeners themselves. Isaiah had gone from being a beautiful artist to a prophet, painting a far-more realistic picture than anyone wanted to see. His final message: God wants you to change your lives. And no one likes to change.

❦28❦

Therefore I tell you, the kingdom of God will be taken away from you and given to a people that produce the fruits of the kingdom.

MATTHEW 21:43

In the cool of the evening, in the temple precincts of Jerusalem, they heard His voice. Who was this Jesus who spoke to them? He spoke to them of a vineyard, but spiced his story with tales of treachery and intrigue, even murder. And so they listened, absorbing His words as if they were a beautiful, dramatic piece of music. But then the composer of this symphony changed keys abruptly. These people, the ones who killed the son of the vineyard owner—that was this group of listeners. His final message: God wants you to change your lives. And so, challenged to change, the people turned their backs on Him and His beautiful words. We all know that we need to change in order to grow and to move on, but it can sometimes be so painful.

❦29❦

All is change; all yields its place and goes.

EURIPIDES

There can be a real comfort in grief. In a world where so much changes, where people are born and die every day, there can be a strange comfort in merely sticking with grief which always remains. "It's my suffering," we seem to say. "At least I can count on it."

But to truly grow, to truly allow life to triumph over death, we must pick ourselves up and move on. The pain, the sorrow, the regret—all of these remain somehow a part of us, but they are transformed into avenues of possibility, of hope. Isaiah and the prophets, Jesus Christ—they were all right: God wants us to change our lives. And though this change, this moving on, is painful, we can always turn to their words and examples to help show us the way.

❧ 30 ❧

Lord for your faithful people, life has changed, not ended.

FROM THE PREFACE OF THE
RITE OF CHRISTIAN BURIAL

At the visitation for my mother, my father, in what had to be one of the most difficult tasks of his life, approached the casket holding the hand of his seven-year-old son and lay that hand on hers, ever the teacher, to show the truth of the body being a vessel for the spirit.

My senses exploded. The sight of my mother; the cold hard feeling of her hand; the overpowering smell of the flowers; the soft music playing in the background; the taste of my tears running into the corner of my mouth. With all of this came a sense of hyper-reality—it was all too real, a bit exaggerated. But I also knew at that moment, as real as her death was, life was a grander reality. Such epiphanies can help make sense of things even to a child.

❧ 31 ❧

We have this hope. A sure and steadfast anchor of the soul.

HEBREWS 6:19

One of the most moving parts of the National Holocaust Memorial and Museum in Washington, DC, is an exhibit called Daniel's Story. This exhibit tells the story of the Holocaust through the eyes of one child. The tone of the exhibit is amazing. No matter what unspeakable tragedies surround Daniel, no matter what he is forced to endure, in every word he utters one can sense through the darkness of his world the unmistakable light of hope. And that this hope comes from one so young says that hope is not something we acquire but something deep within us, innate.

"I've lost hope," we've all felt from time to time, and perhaps rightly so. But we need to remember that if we've lost it, we can find it again. Its light is always with us.

FEBRUARY

❦ 1 ❦

You must sit down, says Love, and taste my meat:
So I did sit and eat.

GEORGE HERBERT

The most severe guilt often surrounds the pain of loss. We can be plagued by unkind words or actions that we directed at loved ones who are no longer with us. Their silence seems to indict us. We can have difficulty letting go of hurts that we may have experienced at their hands, and we long to tell them how much they hurt us, at the same time feeling bad for thinking ill of the dead.

We must be confident that the love that can bring forth a baby from the womb of a virgin; the love that can cause the deaf to hear, the blind to see, and the lame to leap like stags; the love that can bring life forth where there had only before been death can vanquish the hunger of guilt and remorse.

❦ 2 ❦

The march of the human mind is slow.

EDMUND BURKE

We can look back at our lives and see the hand of God in the people we've encountered, the struggles we've endured, and in the joys we've celebrated. At those times we can begin to wrap our minds around the notion of God's plan, of life in the image of Christ. It can, at times, start to make sense to us.

And then something can happen (usually something bad) so our minds and hearts can be hurled back into confusion. "I don't get it, God. How is this supposed to help me? Why did this have to happen?" And in moments such as these it is as if the insight is replaced by doubt and confusion.

Our minds can be attuned to God again. It just takes some time.

❧ 3 ❧

Your heavenly Father knows that you need all these things.

MATTHEW 6:32

People spend a great deal of time worrying. There can be worthwhile worries: Will I make enough money to support my family? Will I have enough to eat? Will I be able to move on with my life after this tragedy? And there are worries that are less pressing: What will I wear to the party? What if I don't get the promotion? Will I be able to afford that new sports car?

Because life is filled with all kinds of worries, it is important to be able to distinguish between those really important questions and those questions that are really not all that significant. And the answer to all of the really pressing questions in life, the destination for all our searching, is God—plain and simple. Often we'll find He's answered the question before we ask it, if we pay attention.

❧ 4 ❧

Sometimes, when one person is missing,
the whole world seems depopulated.

LAMARTINE

When the bells tolled announcing the death of Father Theodore, I felt cheated. He had been working in South Dakota for some time, and I hadn't seen him in years. "I never got to say goodbye," I lamented over and over again. His absence suddenly seeemed more acute because of its finality.

But since then, every time I laugh at an outrageous story about him, every time my lips curl into a smile at the mere thought of him, and every time, in the midst of the laughter and the smiles I sense the familiar pang of loss, I realize I am saying goodbye. It's just that goodbyes take time.

❧ 5 ❧

Be perfect, therefore,
as your heavenly Father is perfect.

MATTHEW 5:48

Who among us is perfect? Who among us can even hope to strive for real perfection? No one of course, for the limits of our humanity are all too real.

But we can hope to be perfected. We can hope that graces we receive in life will strengthen us, draw us closer to that perfection which the Father possesses. But if we truly desire to be perfected, we must see all that life has to offer as grace, as a possible means toward that perfected-ness. All that life has to offer, not just what we like. This is difficult to do, because after all, no one is perfect.

❧ 6 ❧

Why do you worry about clothing?
Consider the lilies of the field, how they grow;
they neither toil nor spin.
Yet, I tell you, even Solomon in all his glory
was not clothed like one of these.

MATTHEW 6:28-29

Recently I asked a group of students what they most wanted out of life. The list was astounding in its detail and a bit disheartening in its content: cars, homes, stereos, in-home theatre systems, and—of course—high-paying jobs that would ensure all of this stuff. I was about to preach to them about what really matters in life when I noticed one of them eyeing my new pair of shoes. We all know that money (and the things it can bring us) won't buy us happiness. But all too often (especially when sadness hits) I think we all try to rent it a bit, shutting out the recognition that the true stuff of happiness (time, support, love) can be purchased at no cost whatsoever.

❧ 7 ❧

All the ends of the earth have seen the victory of our God.

PSALM 98

To get from the Monastery to my office, I have to walk through our church—something I do numerous times each day. At every trek through the church, I take a moment to bow at the altar (the symbol of Christ in the church), but I rarely notice anything else. I don't pay attention to the beautiful marble floors, the soaring Romanesque arches, the magnificent stained-glass windows. Such amazing brilliance is all around me but, because of eyes made dull by routine, I hardly ever notice it.

The entire world has seen the salvation and glory of God and, all too often, because of eyes made dull by routine, stress, suffering or pain, we hardly ever notice it. Just because we fail to notice it doesn't mean it's not there.

❧ 8 ❧

All men who live with any degree of serenity
live by some assurance of grace.

REINHOLD NIEBUHR

When a monk is dying, the rest of us take turns sitting with him so he will not die alone. And so it was my turn to sit with Brother Casimir in what ended up being the last morning of his life here on earth. At first, the heat of the room, the drone of the oxygen machine, the antiseptic smell, and the labored breathing made me feel crowded, claustrophobic. But the longer I sat there, uncomfortable, I began to realize that even more than all of the stuff crowding the room (and specifically because of all that stuff) grace was powerfully present as well. We can try to crowd it out of our lives, but it just won't go away.

❧ 9 ❧

*Jesus was led up by the Spirit into the wilderness
to be tempted by the devil.*

MATTHEW 4:1

He could have given in and things might have gone better for him. If Jesus would have turned stones into bread, thrown Himself from the highest point of the temple, and taken command of all the kingdoms, surely more people would have believed in Him, more people would have acknowledged Him as God. And this Kingdom of God that He kept preaching about would have been realized then and there, instead of everyone waiting for its fulfillment the way we still do today. Yes, I suppose, He could have given in, but He didn't. Because you see, to give in would have meant that Jesus was buying into what the world thought He should be. He was instead about his Father's business, a business that—much to the confusion and consternation of the world—said that life could actually come from death.

❧ 10 ❧

Every charitable act is a stepping stone toward heaven.

HENRY WARD BEECHER

During my sophomore year in college my classmates and I were conscripted to volunteer for supper service at St. John's Bread Line. We were positively glowing with that good feeling one gets when one feels really useful, genuinely needed. How wonderful we felt to be putting our faith into action.

The more we worked there, however (and very hard work it ended up being), the more the distinction between the ministers and the ones being ministered to became blurred. We soon became powerfully aware that these holy and righteous acts of ours (which we imagined were inching us closer to Heaven) were indeed opportunities to share in the wonders of humanity—good and ill—and thus see a little bit of Heaven here on earth.

❧ 11 ❧

He went to the first [son] and said,
"Son, go and work in the vineyard today."
[The son] answered, "I will not,"
but later he changed his mind and he went.

MATTHEW 21:28-30

Maybe his intentions weren't so good, this first son. Work in the vineyard? "I will not." Maybe he didn't need temptation to present itself to him maybe he already knew there was a pretty-fun world outside of the drudgery of the vineyard and he wanted to be a part of it all. And it could be that he had no intention whatsoever of working in that vineyard, thinking instead of the great possibilities that existed for him. Maybe his intentions weren't so good, but then again maybe he knew all along in the back of his mind that the vineyard was where he belonged. And just maybe after his, "I will not," he headed that direction anyway. Who knows? A lot can happen on the way to the vineyard.

❧ 12 ❧

The Father went to the second [son] and said the same;
[this son] answered, "I go, sir," but did not go.

MATTHEW 21:30

Maybe his intentions were good, this second son. Mindful of his duties, obedient to his father, maybe he really did intend to go to the vineyard and work. "I go sir." But who knows? Maybe there were people in the vineyard he didn't want to see. Maybe he didn't want to risk being stung by the bees that surrounded the sweet excess of the fruit. Maybe he began to think about how hard he had worked in the vineyard the last time he was there, and decided that he was too tired. Maybe his intentions were good, but who knows? A lot can happen on the way to the vineyard.

❧ 13 ❧

They shall plant vineyards and eat their fruit.

ISAIAH 65:21

All too often, especially when we are enjoying periods of prosperity and serenity, we make ourselves believe that life should be this prosperous and serene all the time. But the fact of the matter remains that, even though life can be delicious and sweet indeed, it takes effort and action to help make it that way. Living, grieving, learning, growing, loving— all these elements of life's vineyard need tending to. And there will be times when we fear the exhaustion or the bee stings that can be part of it all. But even though we may fear these things, we need to be resolute in our desire for the Kingdom, because not only is the fruit worth the toil, but the trip there can be pretty amazing as well. A lot can happen on the way to the vineyard.

❧ 14 ❧

*Jesus said to his disciples: "Peace I leave with you;
my peace I give to you."*

JOHN 14:27

Elsewhere He spoke of a peace where the closest family members would be divided against one another. It begs the question, "Do we really want His peace?" If this is what His gift of peace means, then perhaps our tendency is to want to return the gift or exchange it for something less taxing. The world is filled with enough division and sorrow as it is; why go looking for more?

The Lord's notion of peace is much deeper than just a nice calm or a lack of friction in our lives. His peace makes us aware that no matter what, He will not abandon us. He will not leave us to struggle in this world alone, even in the face of the sorrow that can come about as a result of our following Him in this mysterious way of peace. It's a strange gift, this peace, but in the end it is the most precious gift we could hope for.

❧ 15 ❧

The soul is healed by being with children.

FYODOR DOSTOEVSKY

After the funeral of my Uncle Billy, our family gathered at my cousin Diane's house for the obligatory post-funeral food fest. The mood, understandably, was somber. Adults sat around in clutches, passing the time of day, but not really talking, as adults are often wont to do. Every sad, exaggerated pause was avoided by a phrase such as, "This potato salad is the best! What's your secret?" All of a sudden, in the midst of it all, my niece Abigail burst noisily into the room, her cheeks flushed with the excitement of her latest game. "Abby!" her mother reprimanded as the other parents looked on with knowing glances. I set aside my fried chicken and green bean casserole and followed the little piper out of the room, certain she was on to something.

❧ 16 ❧

Everyone should carefully observe which way his heart draws him, and then choose that way with all his strength.

HASIDIC SAYING

I was in a park in downtown St. Louis one day, on a break from a conference I was attending, and I encountered a truly wonderful sight. Standing in the middle of one of the fountain pools there, looking up to the heavens with a beatific smile, heartily enjoying a bratwurst dripping with mustard, was a man in a very formal business suit, socks and shoes removed and pants rolled up to his knees. "That man obviously has problems," the woman standing next to me said, observing the curious scene, and she was probably right. But the more I reflected on it, I was touched by the sheer joy obviously bursting forth from his heart. I began to think that he quite possibly had the solution.

❧17❧

He breathed on them and said to them, "Receive the Holy Spirit."

JOHN 20:22

Though fear is human, the overcoming of fear is divine. Jesus Himself stood in the midst of frightened human beings, and all the fearful thoughts were replaced by thoughts of praise and awe: He had indeed risen, as He said He would. And even if they had plenty of good reasons to fear, Jesus put their confusing lives into perspective: "Peace be with you," He said, and then He breathed on them, the cool wonder of His breath overtaking them and quenching the heat of the fear that was so oppressively present in that room.

When we suffer one loss in our lives, it is understandable to fear another. But the same promise of peace and the Spirit that tempered the fear of the early disciples can temper our fear as well and replace its uncomfortable heat with a refreshing breath, with the coolness of an empty tomb.

❧18❧

And he was transfigured before them, and his face shone like the sun, and his clothes became dazzling white.

MATTHEW 17:2

The days are getting longer. Each morning when I wake up, I notice more and more light in the sky, more streaks of color in the East. The light cheers me and warms my heart. Daily I am able to be surrounded more by its wonder, its warmth, its promise, its hope. I think this is the most compelling aspect of the light—it can be a vessel of such hope. Even at times when so much darkness can fill our lives, bringing with it the appearance of an unending night, the light comes, blinding in its hope, radiant in its promise. That same light, that same promise, that same hope is extended to us as well. If we truly hope in God, if we trust His promises to us, then no matter how much darkness reigns in our lives, no matter how often we view our world through the dreary shades of night, we too can be transfigured.

❧ 19 ❧

Everyone who hears these words of mine and acts on them
will be like the wise man who built his house on rock.

MATTHEW 7:24

Sometimes we put our trust in possessions: "If only I had this or that I would be able to shake the emptiness and sadness that seem to frequently crowd my life." Sometimes we can put our trust in other people: "All I need is to have a better relationship with (you fill in the blank) and my problems will go away." Sometimes we can put our trust in work: "If I just reach the next level of my job, I will be able to relax and really enjoy life." Sometimes we put our trust in the Lord: "If only I can grow closer to Jesus, my life will make more sense."

We don't need a book to tell us which of these things are solid foundations and which aren't. But we happen to have a book: the Bible.

❧ 20 ❧

Is anything too wonderful for the Lord to do?

GENESIS 18:14

The giggle gave her away. Sarah, quite old and well past childbearing age, overheard three mysterious strangers tell her old husband Abraham that by next year she would have a son. How preposterous a notion. And so Sarah, eyes rolling, head shaking, laughed at the absurdity of it all and the Lord heard her giggle.

He had the last laugh of course, because a year later, when Abraham was 100 years old and Sarah somewhere near that, little Isaac came onto the scene.

The moral: Never underestimate just how far our absurd God will go to show His love for us. He'll always have the last laugh.

❧ 21 ❧

We are astonished at thought,
but sensation is equally wonderful.

VOLTAIRE

My sister has started wearing the same perfume that my Aunt Katie wore when I was a child. I haven't seen Aunt Katie in years, but one hug from my sister and it all comes back to me: lying on the couch in her house, wrapped in an orange and black afghan, her poodle Mitzie resting nearby. They happen every now and then, these "scentories": I smell cinnamon and suddenly I'm sitting at the counter, watching Grandma make her famous rolls; I smell leather and I'm sitting on my Grandpa Lewis' lap in his big old chair; I smell leaves burning and I'm playing in the leaves while my mother watches from a lawn chair. For a moment they're all here with me again, and although it makes me sad, I can't deny that there is joy as well. And I breathe it in.

❧ 22 ❧

Look to him, and be radiant.

PSALM 34

John Fisher, we are told, recited this line just before he was martyred. It seems he was able to see the rays of the sun peeking over the shape of the gallows that would soon hold his body, and he saw in that sun the true Light of the World, the Light that he had every confidence would snatch him from the darkness of death.

Such inspiration is not uncommon on the lips of martyrs. And that which has enabled countless people over the centuries to view death as an avenue to something greater is deep within our hearts as well. We need to call upon our radiant God to help us find it, even when we face life's little martyrdoms at an alarming rate.

❧ 23 ❧

For in the dew of little things
the heart finds its morning and is refreshed.

KAHLIL GIBRAN

"Watch this!" four-year-old Abigail shouted as she prepared to mount her bicycle without training wheels for the first time. And down the sidewalk she rode, an enormous smile on her cherubic face. We all cheered wildly. Car after car drove past, and not one driver seemed to pay the scene any mind, doubtless involved in their own thoughts, brows furrowed with more serious matters. Those of us present for Abigail's triumph knew that it wasn't an earth-shattering event of global importance. But at the time it seemed pretty close.

❧ 24 ❧

But Lot's wife, behind him, looked back,
and she was turned into a pillar of salt.

GENESIS 19:26

She has become the poster-child of regret. Frozen for all time, her lips beginning to trace the words, "What if?" she stands as a symbol for all of us who have wondered, from time to time, if we said or did the right thing. Maybe she worried that there were those in her doomed city who would perish before she had a chance to tell them how important they were to her. Who knows what she was thinking as the taste of regret turned salty upon her lips.

We can learn two important lessons from this woman. First of all, we learn that regret rarely allows us to move forward but instead can freeze us in attitudes of hurt and pain. Secondly, Lot's wife teaches us that we should be extra vigilant in living our lives so that regret is not part of them.

❧25❧

Blessed are the poor in spirit, for theirs is the kingdom of heaven.

MATTHEW 5:3

"Be strong, he would have wanted it that way." Or, "That which doesn't kill us only makes us stronger." In times of sorrow we can readily give into the notion that we always have to be strong, we always need to have our act together, we always have to know all the answers. And from this storehouse of strength, somehow we can move on, can function, can do all the things we need to do.

In opposition to this is Jesus' idea that those who aren't always strong, those who struggle and wonder, those whose souls know the emptiness and poverty of loss—somehow these are the ones who are strong, who are blessed. Perhaps what we perceive as strength isn't really strength after all.

❧26❧

Blessed are those who mourn, for they will be comforted.

MATTHEW 5:4

In all of sacred scripture there are perhaps no other words as courageous in their simplistic optimism than these. How, we might venture to ask, are the mourners to be comforted? Jesus doesn't answer. He simply moves on to the next Beatitude, leaving the question hanging in the air like a fog.

But the answer is there—perhaps not as concretely as we would like—but it is there nonetheless. Because who among us has not mourned? Who among us has not felt the depths of our heart pierced with sadness? And that which has allowed humanity to keep moving despite the pain for millennia is what will somehow bring us to the realization that we are blessed indeed.

❧ 27 ❧

Blessed are the meek, for they will inherit the earth.

MATTHEW 5:5

It's a little hard to swallow sometimes, this notion of the meek inheriting the earth. One can look around and see powerful, corrupt tycoons and rulers of peoples quite literally taking what they want while many others suffer and go without in quiet desperation. The meek get trampled while the strong seem to do most of the inheriting.

But in the quiet simplicity of meek hearts can rest something so powerful that the leaders of this world are powerless in comparison. And that is love, pure and simple. Love which can turn hearts of stone into hearts of flesh. Love which can give seekers their ultimate destination. Love which even death cannot destroy. If we look around and see people who meekly live their lives in accordance with this love, we'll find that the earth is already theirs.

❧ 28 ❧

Blessed are those who hunger and thirst for righteousness,
for they will be satisfied.

MATTHEW 5:6

I learned that righteousness means acting in accord with God's law, seeking what God seeks, desiring what God desires. And this definition can be a bit hazy at times. How can we know what God's law is when so many people interpret it in so many ways? How can we know what God seeks when the searching of so many people leads them in such varying directions? How can we know what God desires when so many people brandish the words "It's God's will" like swords, cutting down those who may see God's desires elsewhere? Confusion is understandable.

There is no confusion, however, in this: God loves us passionately. And perhaps what God desires more than anything is that we know this love and allow it to shape and mold our lives.

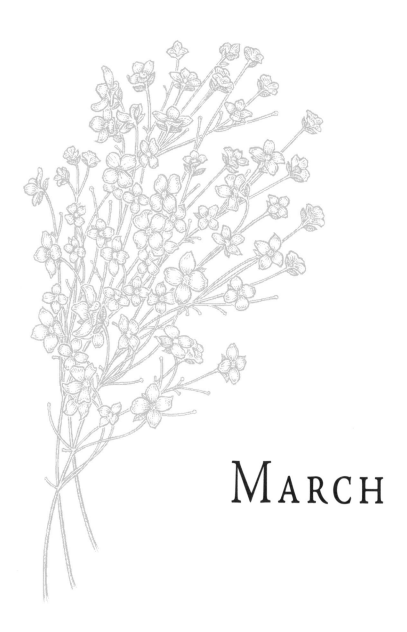

MARCH

❧ 1 ❧

Blessed are the merciful, for they will obtain mercy.

MATTHEW 5:7

When I made the decision to volunteer my time at Bonaventure House, a residence on Chicago's North Side for people with AIDS, I was amazed at the resistance I encountered from people based mainly on ignorance of how the disease was transmitted and the possibility of "catching it" somehow. The most distressing line, though, came from a relative of mine: "Why would you waste your time with those people? They got what they deserved."

A statement like this belies ignorance of a basic tenet of humanity: We are all connected somehow. The suffering of one person affects the whole group even if we can't always see it. And if we don't show mercy to all people who share in the wonders of humanity, we just may find that we will have a hard time feeling that merciful connection when we need it most.

❧ 2 ❧

Blessed are the pure in heart, for they will see God.

MATTHEW 5:8

Not too long after my mother died, I remember my father's mentally-challenged brother coming to stay with us. Whenever sadness would overwhelm me, Uncle Billy set me on his lap, showed me his pocket watch and harmonica, and rubbed my head. My grief would remain, of course, but its hold on me was significantly tempered by this simple, beautiful man and his gentle ways.

We sometimes look for great revelations, for instant insights as to why God allows certain things to happen in the world, things that bring about sadness. More often than not, these questions go unanswered, or they don't get answered in the way we'd prefer. But if we look hard enough in the loving caresses of humanity, the extraordinary presence of God is manifest.

❧ 3 ❧

Blessed are the peacemakers,
for they will be called children of God.

MATTHEW 5:9

Regret is one of the most tragic human emotions. Thoughts such as, "If only I would have," "I should have done..." and "Why didn't I ever say..." race through our minds, causing a battle between what should have been and what really happened. And, as in all battles, the wounds can be significant.

But the peace for which we often pray, the peace that makes us blessed, can begin to heal the wounds even if the scars remain. In moving from what should have been to what is, and accepting what is, we dodge the barbed arrows of regret and find the balm of acceptance.

❧ 4 ❧

Go, eat your bread with enjoyment
and drink your wine with a merry heart.

ECCLESIASTES 9:7

When I was growing up, the kitchen was the place where visitors were received. Stories told, sorrows shared, gossip exchanged, jokes recounted—it all happened around the kitchen table, usually with a fresh pot of coffee and some rolls at hand. And when I think about it, the kitchen is the perfect place for this activity. Because just as there is something ultimately satisfying about filling our empty stomachs with food and drink, there is also something wonderful about filling our lives with friendship. Sometimes friendship can be needed more than food and drink; and sometimes it is more satisfying too.

❦ 5 ❦

I, the Lord, have spoken and will act, says the Lord.

EZEKIEL 37:14

God said there would be light and there was light. God said Adam wouldn't be alone and He created Eve. God said Abraham would be the father of a great nation and he was. God said, "I will be born into your midst" and He was. God said, "I will teach you what love is all about"; God said, "I will suffer and die that you may live."

So when we find ourselves doubting, when we find that we are angry or bewildered by God's apparent callousness, when we wonder if He really cares at all, it does us good to go over His track record and realize He hasn't failed us yet.

❦ 6 ❦

I will not leave you until I have done what I promised you.

GENESIS 28:15

Although we may want to, we can't know all the answers. And since there are things we don't know, we need to rely on faith—pure and simple. What if there is nothing after we die? Faith says: "He who believes in me shall never die." What if we can't find our way? Faith says: "I am the Way." What if the sorrow never departs us? Faith says: "I will change your mourning into dancing."

The words of the Scriptures, the examples of our fellow Christians throughout the ages, the tradition of the Church all point to the answers of the questions that can plague us in life. But in the end, it is Faith that enables us to see we are not left alone, that all of God's promises will be fulfilled. "Lord, increase our faith," is an earnest cry for answers.

❧ 7 ❧

Praise God from whom all blessings flow.

THOMAS KEN

Many of us can't read these words without hearing an accompanying tune. This doxology summarizes our entire relationship with God. How often have we heard or even sung these words and not given them much thought? How often has the sword of familiarity cut through our ability to hear these words and recognize in them an amazing truth: Absolutely everything we have, everything that sustains us, everything that allows us to live—all of it comes from God.

What a reason to praise God. What a reason to shake off the torpor of familiarity and search for meaning anew.

❧ 8 ❧

Jesus began to weep.

JOHN 11:35

I once heard a good-intentioned minister say to a grieving widow, "Too many tears send the message that we doubt the resurrection of the dead." I didn't correct him (he had, after all, been in the ministry before I was even born) but I couldn't help thinking how offtrack he was. Jesus' mourning of his friend Lazarus gave birth to tears even though He knew for a fact that in a matter of minutes Lazarus would be alive, set free from the darkness of the bonds of the tomb. And so perhaps the tears didn't doubt the resurrection of the dead but acknowledged the toll death takes on the living.

❦ 9 ❦

Winter is come and gone, but grief returns with the revolving year.
PERCY BYSSHE SHELLEY

After her husband Albert died, Queen Victoria followed the custom of the time and began adorning herself in the black of mourning. But when the acceptable time of mourning came to an end, she continued to drape her ample frame in black as if to say she would never be finished mourning the one she loved so dearly.

Time may dull the pain of loss, but pain cannot be eradicated. And so as one year turns into another, we need to realize each new season may bring about memories and reflections that make the loss seem present in new ways. Our task then is not to get over it somehow as if it's inappropriate to feel sad; rather our task is to acknowledge the grief but make sure we don't allow it to stop us completely.

❦ 10 ❦

Beauty will save the world.
FYDOR DOSTEOVSKY

Being from the Midwest, my first view of the ocean (the Atlantic, to be specific) occurred when I was ten years old. We had been driving in the car for what seemed like years to my young mind, and the scene in the car was typical vacation fare: My brother annoyed me by crossing the imaginary line I had drawn in the back seat; I annoyed my father with the interminable, "Are we there yet?"; my father annoyed my stepmother by not asking for directions when we were clearly lost.

And suddenly in the midst of all this the ocean came into view. The bickering stopped as we were struck silent by the majesty of the Atlantic. It all returned of course—the annoying, unpleasant realities of life—but for a moment we were able to rise above it by drinking in the wonder of the ocean's beauty.

❦ 11 ❦

For in Christ's coach saints sweetly sing
As they to glory ride therein.

EDWARD TAYLOR

Most of us, if asked where we stood on the saint-to-sinner scale, would most likely place ourselves closer to the sinner side, perhaps rightly so. But the scale is not as broad as we think, and the difference between the two not so grand that Christ could not bridge it with His outstretched arms.

So we can dare to hope that not only will we one day ride to glory, singing with the other saints, but also that among the number will be those whom we loved.

❦ 12 ❦

I always do the first line well, but have trouble doing the others.

MOLIÈRE

"It was a dark and stormy night," countless authors have begun, only to have the story fall apart in the second paragraph. Even if we don't write ourselves, this phenomenon is not unknown to us. We have the best intentions of beginning something, of knowing what is the best course of action, but for all our good intentions we sometimes have difficulty following through.

Knowing that this is a part of our human condition can help us. Because when we have made up our mind how the story should go, but can't seem to follow through, we can always go back to the beginning. Bit by bit, with patience in ourselves and with others, we begin to have the strength to move on from the first line, to see beyond the dark and stormy night to the bright and clear day that follows.

❧ 13 ❧

They were amazed, saying, "What sort of man is this,
that even the winds and the sea obey him?"

MATTHEW 8:27

The winds assailed, blowing fiercely, chafing skin, quickening hearts, blustering fear. The waters threatened, soaking skin, quickening hearts, saturating fear. And then, in the midst of it all (the boat nearly capsized), He stood and took the sea and winds to task. And then the winds and water calmed, skin feeling refreshed, hearts slowing, fear evaporating. Who is this that can stand in the midst of elements quite beyond our feeble control and take them to task?

It is the same one who can still calm the storms of our own lives, who still has the ability in the midst of a whirlwind to take it all to task—the suffering, sadness, doubt, anguish and numbness—and say to them, "You will not have the final say here, I will!"

We need only to get in the boat with Him.

❧ 14 ❧

Into each life some rain must fall,
some days must be dark and dreary.

HENRY WADSWORTH LONGFELLOW

I had a professor once say that people who wish for great wealth and happiness will never be satisfied because they'll never be wealthy and happy enough. Who knows if this is really true, but I think there is some wisdom to it especially on the happiness end. In times of great elation we sometimes find ourselves wondering why life can't be like this all the time, or at least more often. But the reality is that this sort of unending bliss is just not possible.

And so, when we have our times of inestimable happiness, we need to constantly be aware that it is a gift and, most likely, a short-lived one at that. But so too in our dark days do we need to be aware that this cannot last forever, and so accept the rainfall with resignation while at the same time always looking for the sun.

❧ 15 ❧

I will be like the dew to Israel: he shall blossom like the lily.

HOSEA 14:5

Lilies are a wonderful flower and it is no surprise they have become synonymous with the joy of Easter. Their scent is intoxicating; I love to walk into our church Easter morning and breathe the scent of the lilies mingled with incense and candle wax.

Perhaps more amazing than these potted, planned lilies are the surprise lilies that seem to spring from nowhere. Nestled amid trees or in open fields, they spring from the earth as a testimony to the surprise of the empty tomb, to the surprise of a God who at any time and in any place can spring up in our lives, intoxicating us with His beauty.

❧ 16 ❧

This is courage in a man: to bear unflinchingly what heaven sends.

EURIPIDES

When I was young I loved to spend wintry Saturday afternoons watching old movies on Channel 11. Ordinarily it was action-packed fare: Errol Flynn as a swashbuckling pilot, James Cagney as a gangster with a heart of gold, Johnny Weismuller swinging on his vines, John Wayne astride his horse. I was captivated by these men and the courage they exhibited in fighting off adversaries. I hoped one day to be as courageous as they, to lead a life filled with such intrigue and excitement.

The older I get, the more I realize courage bears less resemblance to these figures than it does to my Gramps, quietly playing solitaire in a kitchen left empty by my Grandma's passing. We needn't look to a pirate's ship or the Old West to see true courage; we need only look to the strength that allows us to move forward in life.

❦17❦

No doubt my poetry errs on the side of oddness.

GERARD MANLEY HOPKIN

Many of the great people of history were, in their own times, quite misunderstood. Jesus was constantly challenged by the Pharisees about things He said and did that just didn't seem to fit with the prevailing religious thought of the day. How odd. Francis of Assisi stripped himself naked and gave all his clothes to his father in the town square. How odd. Bernadette of Lourdes kept having conversations with a beautiful woman that no one else seemed to be able to see. How odd.

And so, if others try to make us feel that there is only one way to pray, to grieve, to express ourselves, we need not automatically give in to their way of thinking. God who is infinite can and does help us in ways that are as different as we are different. How odd.

If others try to make us feel
that there is only one way to pray, to grieve, to express ourselves,
we need not automatically give in to their way of thinking.

❧18❧

Pain is deeper than all thought; laughter is higher than all pain.

ELBERT HUBBARD

Father Julian has the uncanny ability to make me laugh at the most serious times—usually when we are in church. We will be listening to a solemn reading, the account of someone's martyrdom, for example; I'll look up across the choir, catch his eye, and the slightest of gestures—a smirk, a raised eyebrow—will for some reason always bring about laughter in me—laughter, of course, that I have to suppress because it is not appropriate to laugh in church.

Or so they say.

I'm not so sure. The world is filled with enough sorrow and tragedy and routine and seriousness. Sometimes laughter is the only thing that can cover all of that and raise our low spirits. And if raising low spirits isn't of God, I don't know what is.

❧19❧

I am sending you out like sheep, into the midst of wolves.

MATTHEW 10:16

The world can be a dangerous place. In addition to violence, disasters and accidents that can season the world in which we live, so too can human misunderstanding, sorrow, division and enmity. It can be a natural response at times to want to flee the world, to remove ourselves from those things which seem to take their toll on us. But it is specifically into the world—and all that it holds for us—that the Lord sends us. It is specifically in the world that, even though we may encounter grief and loss and suffering, we also encounter the grace to overcome it. Such is the promise of the Good Shepherd who won't let the wolves of the world overtake us, His sheep.

❧20

Come, gentle Spring! Ethereal mildness, come.

JAMES THOMSON

The winter can become a habit, a strange solace in and of itself. Wrapped against the blistering breezes, shut away from the ice and snow, steeled against the night we can become so accustomed to the season's battles that we forget to look for the spring's relief. If nothing else, we can at least count on the harshness of winter which offers few surprises.

Not so with spring. Spring finds flowers popping up where barren, icy earth once lay. Spring finds life bursting forth from its hibernation, scratching its belly and stretching in the wonder of it all. Spring finds surprise everywhere we look—even within ourselves.

❧21❧

It is always springtime in a heart filled with love.

SAINT JOHN VIANNEY

We all know, on a rational level, that spring follows winter. We can experience each year the gloomy darkness of days giving way to the lengthening of light, the cold air giving way to warmth, the barren ground giving way to delicious life.

But the transition from the winter of our discontent to the spring of hope and promise can be much more difficult to make. How can it be, we wonder, that a heart so painfully hard and cold due to loss can ever be warm again? The answer is through love—and only through love. Because only by being mindful of the love that was, the love that is, and the love that will be can hearts broken be made whole and wondrous life burst forth from what once was cold and dark.

❧22❧

Now when Jesus heard [of the death of John the Baptist],
he withdrew from there in a boat to a deserted place by himself.

MATTHEW 14:13

His cousin was dead. Their relationship began with the Baptizer dancing in his mother's womb at the presence of his cousin also in the womb. Their relationship was sealed in the Jordan when the two of them swirled into the waters. And their relationship was ended with a mother's vengeful spite—and a girl's frenzied dance. And to make sense of it all, to express the grief that tore His heart, Jesus wanted to be alone.

But after this, the Gospel tells us, He went on to feed five-thousand people. Perhaps He realized that, although the amazing relationship begun so long ago had ended, there were still people around who needed to be fed. Perhaps He knew that in remembering the dead He could not neglect the needs of the living.

❧23❧

But Mary treasured all these words
and pondered them in her heart.

LUKE 2:19

My Gramps was a real storyteller, and I used to sit in fascination while he recounted stories of his colorful life over a cup of coffee and a game of solitaire. Gramps' stories were real, and I learned a great deal about life and who I am while drinking in the wonder of his memories.

Memories, it's true, can be painful. But it is important, in trying to heal our grief, that we don't allow ourselves to keep them only in our hearts. Because when we remember someone somehow they are still with us. And if we can recognize this presence, then death will never have the final word for the story will continue in us.

❦ 24 ❦

But the angel said to him, "Do not be afraid, Zechariah,
for your prayer has been heard.
Your wife Elizabeth will bear you a son,
and you will name him John."

LUKE 1:13

How amazing it happened, how seemingly impossible. Zechariah and Elizabeth, now advancing in years, had most likely resigned themselves to the fact that they would have no children. In a place and time where it was felt that if you couldn't have children you must have done something wrong, they had quietly endured the talk, the pity. And with each passing year the hope that had burned so brightly at the beginning of their life together grew more and more dim. And then it happened. Elizabeth, thought to be sterile, was pregnant, and the hope that had been all but extinguished now grew and blazed inside of her. How amazing that it happened, how seemingly impossible. But nothing is impossible with God.

❦ 25 ❦

Mary said to the angel,
"How can this be, since I am a virgin?"

LUKE 1:34

How amazing that it happened, how seemingly impossible. Mary, a young girl, was visited by an angel of God with an astounding message: God wanted to be born into the world and into frail humanity. And to help bring this about, he chose a young girl and asked her to agree to this wonder, this confusion. The young girl said "yes" to the will of God and the womb of a virgin now nurtured a child. How amazing that it happened, how seemingly impossible. But nothing is impossible with God.

❦26❦

For nothing will be impossible with God.

LUKE 1:37

Perhaps the stories of Mary and Elizabeth have lost their power to captivate, to make us aware of the possibilities that exist in the seemingly impossible. This is sad, for we frequently need to be reminded of these possibilities, to see the seemingly impossible tasks of healing and forgiveness as possibilities. Because the same God who allowed a barren old woman to conceive, the same God who could bring forth a baby from the womb of a virgin, can manifest in us impossible possibilities, if only we believe like Elizabeth and trust like Mary. We can achieve amazing things. Because nothing is impossible with God.

❦27❦

And silence, like a poultice, comes
To heal the blows of sound.

OLIVER WENDELL HOLMES

One of the things about monastic life which people are most the curious about is our emphasis on silence. We eat breakfast in silence. We don't speak in the hallways. We eat dinner without speaking and while listening to a book being read. We don't talk before church in the morning or after 10:00 p.m. at night. The emphasis on silence for monks is usually linked to interior stillness so as to better hear the voice of God.

But silence—not just for monks, but for anyone—can also help us put things in perspective. When the world is assaulting us with noise, it is in true silence that we can begin to hear what is really important, what is really touching us at that moment, what we need to do. And what is this perspective, this insight, if not the voice of God?

❧ 28 ❧

Si monumentum requiris circumspice
[If you would see the man's monument, look around.]
—INSCRIPTION IN SAINT PAUL'S CATHEDRAL, LONDON
WRITTEN BY THE SON OF ARCHITECT SIR CHRISTOPHER WREN

To most tourists in London it is a destination, the beautiful Saint Paul's Cathedral, the site of the wedding of Charles and Diana all those years ago. It is an amazing building, grand symmetry singing of the perfection of God; high-adorned dome singing of humankind's need to praise God. It is a breathtaking monument to the reality of all things being possible in God.

So too it is a monument to Sir Christopher Wren and, through him, to us all. Not only does it speak of the wonders of God's amazing love, it also speaks of the amazing things we can achieve when we allow ourselves to be enveloped in that love.

❧ 29 ❧

To be able to enjoy one's past life is to live twice.
MARTIAL

During my ordination to the priesthood, as I was lying prostrate on the floor of the cathedral, I was overcome with sadness. There I was on the most important day of my life and two of the most significant people in my life—my mother and my grandmother—were not there to celebrate with me. In the midst of this painful realization, a barrage of images exploded within my mind: My mother opening her gifts at Christmastime; my grandmother enfolding me in the warmth of her fleshy arms; meals where I was happily placed between both of them at the table. And as I heard the cantor recounting the names of great saints who have been witnesses to the faith throughout the ages, I realized that my memory of these two women was a testimony to their witness of the salvific power of love.

❧ 30 ❧

If life had a second edition, how I would correct the proofs.

JOHN CLARE

If only I had said "I love you," or "thank you," or "I appreciate who you are," or "I like who I am when I am with you," or "you are so important to me." If only I hadn't said some of the hateful things I did. If only I had done more for you, with you. If only I hadn't done the things that I did that were hurtful.

Life can be filled with regret, and how nice it would be if we could have that second edition, correct the proofs. But the reality is that we cannot. Those things said and done, things left unsaid and undone, are in the past and there is nothing we can do to change them.

Except, of course, accept their lessons, thus changing the present.

❧ 31 ❧

Heaven is under our feet as well as over our heads.

HENRY DAVID THOREAU

Each year during Lent, one of my resolutions is to take a walk to our cemetery each day. The cemetery is located in a quiet area surrounded by pine trees with a lake nearby. The calmness of it all—the water, the trees, the cool spring air—helps me put things in perspective. I realize that my daily struggles, seemingly so pressing at the time, don't seem so terrible.

It is also clear to me that there, in the dark indifference of the earth, rests the bodies of those who had their own struggles and joys in this same place. They too perhaps walked to this very place, and this place helped them make sense of it all, helped calm them. As my feet trod the grass-covered ground that separates me from them, it dawns on me how really very little separates us at all.

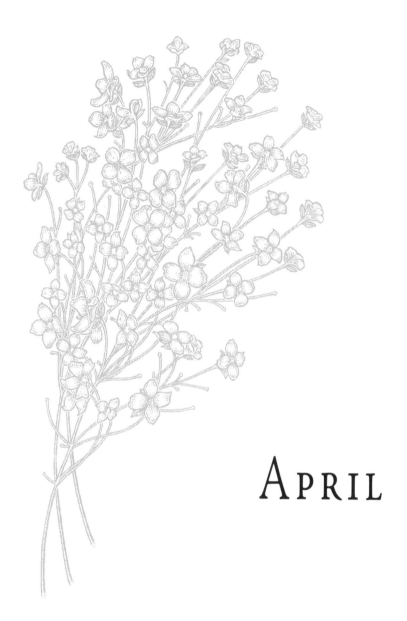

APRIL

❧ 1 ❧

Flowers are lovely; love is flower-like; friendship a sheltering tree.
SAMUEL TAYLOR COLERIDGE

Not too long ago I was at a retreat center in Victoria, Texas, or more accurately, in the middle of nowhere near Victoria, Texas. There was on the grounds the largest oak tree I had ever seen. The caretaker of the center swore that it had been around since the time of Christ, but other estimates put it at maybe 800 years old. Regardless of its true age, it was beautiful. Its gnarled trunk and expansive leafiness was a testimony to steadfastness, permanence.

Coleridge was right in likening friendship to such a tree. There might be people in the world more beautiful, more colorful, more flower-like than our friends. But no one can shelter us the way our friends do.

❧ 2 ❧

[God] said, "Come no closer! Remove the sandals from your feet, for the place on which you stand is holy ground."
EXODUS 3:5

How would we react, standing face-to-face with God, hearing His voice echo like thunder from on high, quaking with fear at the mere thought of being so near the Creator? How would we feel to be so intensely close to the Father of all living things?

We could answer these questions by asking more questions: How do we react when God visits us in the graced moments of our lives? How closely do we listen to His voice when we hear it in those around us, in the still sorrow of our own hearts? How do we feel when the God of all the living things visits us, even in the guise of the sick and dying?

Moses recognized who it was that was speaking to him. Do we?

❦ 3 ❦

They say everything in the world is good for something.

JOHN DRYDEN

I wouldn't describe myself as a pack-rat, but on the other hand I do hate to throw anything away. Rummaging through my office or my room, mindful of needing to get rid of things, I still hesitate to get rid of anything because, even though I'm not a full-fledged pack-rat, I am nonetheless haunted by the Eternal Question of the Pack-Rat: What if I need this later?

There is something to be said for keeping our eyes (and ears and hearts) open for those things (and people) that will be able to help us later—who may even be helping us now.

❦ 4 ❦

Is it not you alone, O Lord? We set our hope on you.

JEREMIAH 14:22

Sometimes it is best not to ask too many questions. Take the people of the prophet Jeremiah's day: Did they really want the Lord to answer the question of where they looked to? The answer was that they were looking everywhere but to the Lord. They looked to idols, as if mere images of gold could fill the emptiness that was within them. They looked to sinful deeds, as if in these actions they would find what they were searching for. They shouldn't have asked if they didn't want to hear the answers.

What about us? Is it to the Lord alone that we look? Do we have the courage to ask this same question?

❧ 5 ❧

But when [Peter] noticed the strong wind,
he became frightened and beginning to sink
he cried out, "Lord, save me!"

MATTHEW 14:29

There had to have been a million voices running through his head: "You can't walk on water." Undeterred, Peter did just that, and sank only when he lost sight of his goal—when he took too much stock in the voices that besieged him.

Similar voices might speak to us as well, the loudest of which are the voices of our own souls: "You can't get over this. It's too much." Undeterred, we need to confidently move forward. And when we feel that we might be sinking in a flood of grief, we must remember to keep our eyes firmly planted on our goal.

❧ 6 ❧

God's finger touched him, and he slept.

ALFRED, LORD TENNYSON

Anyone who knows me well knows that I am not to be disturbed on Sunday afternoons when I retire for a full-force, pajamas-on, under-the-covers nap. The cares and concerns of life don't seem to matter for a couple of hours and my spirit and soul can escape and be refreshed. Everything else is waiting for me when I awake, but for a while I know great peace.

Poets and writers often link death to sleeping and that used to disturb me because it brought with it images of unsuccessfully trying to awaken someone, which is a sad notion. But if I can make myself reflect on the sheer peace of a nap, and imagine awakening not to the struggles of life, but to a continuation of peaceful sleep, then maybe linking death with sleep isn't so bad.

❧ 7 ❧

Jesus said to [Thomas], "I am the way, and the truth, and the life."

JOHN 14:6

Lord, I feel lost. At times I think I know where I am going, that I am on the right path, and at other times I'm not so sure. How can I know where it is I am supposed to be?

"I am the way."

Lord, I feel confused. Things that I have long taken for granted don't seem certain anymore. With so many different messages assailing my ears, how can I be certain which message is the true one?

"I am the truth."

Lord, I feel beaten. Sadness and loss have so clouded my vision that I can no longer see eternity, but am mired instead with viewing only the harsh realities in front of me. With so much death, how can I be certain that everything just doesn't end?

"I am the life."

So many questions. One answer: "I Am."

❧ 8 ❧

At that moment the curtain of the temple
was torn in two, from top to bottom.
The earth shook and the rocks were split.
The tombs were also opened.

MATTHEW 27:51-52

It is the story of one man and the story of all humanity. It is a story that happened in an isolated part of the world and a story the universe could not contain. It is a story, the tragedy of which made the angels weep and caused them also to sing songs of exultation. It is a story of treacherous complexity and yet a story of love, wondrously simple. It is the story of Jesus Christ and yet it is our story: the story of our desires, our failings, our hopes, our sadness, our longings, our lives. It is only through this story that the stories of our lives have any meaning. It is this story that makes us who we are.

❧ 9 ❧

When Jesus had received the wine, he said, "It is finished."
Then he bowed his head, and gave up his spirit.

JOHN 19:30

Good Friday can be a somewhat unnerving day. So many of the images of the Savior with which we surround ourselves stand quiet. Christ the King, Christ the Victor, Christ the Conqueror Over Evil—these are images that comfort us, that make us feel as if things are in control. What images of the Savior do we see around this time of year? That of the suffering servant of Isaiah. We are asked to let go of some of our more comforting images of Jesus and immerse ourselves in the paradox of the Savior of the world submitting Himself to the agony and shame of a common criminal's death, the paradox of the Cross. In one sense, how tragic, how pitiful that cross. But in another sense, the sense of faith, how splendid is that cross! It brings light, not darkness; Paradise, not its loss; life, not death.

❧ 10 ❧

But on the first day of the week, at early dawn, [the women]
came to the tomb, taking the spices that they had prepared.

LUKE 24:1

There are times, in the midst of a world that can confuse and hurt us, when sorrow can be almost soothing. Many things in this world might change, but the real human grief that can affect us all is often constant. Surely this is one of the things that motivated Mary Magdalene and the other women to go to the tomb that first morning. It had been a confusing, painful three days, full of turmoil, and now they were going to the place where they had laid Him, to sit with their sorrow, to be soothed by their tears. Because they knew that even if the last three years of following Him had been a series of oftentimes confusing ups and downs, here, in the cool mist of the morning and in the cool mist of their grief, there was no confusion. There was the ages-old consolation of those who mourn.

❦11❦

They found the stone rolled away from the tomb,
but when they went in, they did not find the body.

LUKE 24:2-3

But the women soon found out that now, in the quiet of death, there was still confusion and turmoil. Because the tomb was not as it had been. The huge stone was rolled away. And so they ran off to the rest of the disciples to see if they could put their confusing world back in order somehow—to bring back the calm. They too were shocked and confused. But John, we read elsewhere, saw and believed. And at that moment he realized: Nothing would ever be calm, nothing would ever be ordinary again. Life as he knew it had changed. Because in a world where darkness was prevalent, light triumphed. In a world where hatred and division were the order of the day, peace was victorious. And in a world where all die, death was rendered impotent.

❦12❦

Protect us by thy might, Great God our King!

SAMUEL FRANCIS SMITH

One night in Texas I was walking along a path back to my cabin when I heard a clicking noise behind me. I turned around and at my feet, apparently as startled as I, was an armadillo. I had never seen one before and I was fascinated by this curious little animal, amazed at how extensive its armor seemed to be.

It helps, especially during times when we feel the most vulnerable, to reflect just how like an armadillo we really are. Instead of hard shells on the outside of our skin, we need to content ourselves with the fact that we have been provided with the armor of friendship, love, memories, joy—all gifts from a God who longs to protect us, curious little animals that we are.

❧ 13 ❧

Wisely, and slow. They stumble that run fast.

WILLIAM SHAKESPEARE

The invention of the microwave has affected the way we live. Gone are the days when making a TV dinner used to take 45 minutes; now it can be dispatched in a mere 10 minutes—Salisbury steak steaming, potatoes a bit crusted, apple cobbler downright molten. Now we expect all things to be dispatched this quickly, giving into the microwave mentality of the harried, slapdash world in which we live.

God's ways are different. God prefers a slow-cooking stew, stirred by a loving cook who wants to make sure that all the ingredients—sweet and bitter—take enough time to really blend. We might not like some of the ingredients, but if we trust the cook we know in the end the taste will be complete—we'll be filled indeed.

❧ 14 ❧

The holiest of all holidays are those
Kept by ourselves in silence and apart;
The secret anniversaries of the heart.

HENRY WADSWORTH LONGFELLOW

My grandmother died on February 14. Each year when the whole country remembers the romantic love that is the staple of Valentine's Day, I remember a different kind of love. I remember her cooking supper as I sat with my Gramps. I remember being enveloped in her soft embrace, while she exclaimed, "You're my baby!" I remember her getting so tickled at something that her laughter would bring about tears and then, apparently on a dime, she would start crying for real, remembering something that saddened her. I remember it all, and I celebrate both the life and the loss. Some would say dwelling year after year on thoughts that ultimately make me sad is tapping into some sort of warped masochism. They can think that. I know I am tapping into holiness.

❧15❧

You have turned my mourning into dancing:
you have taken off my sackcloth and girded me with joy.

PSALM 29

It seems a little far-fetched to me. The slow shuffling of feet weighted down by sadness, replaced by the twirling dance of new life, of hope. The melancholy apparel of sorrowing, replaced by the bright garments of joy. Can it really be this way? It seems awfully difficult to believe that it can.

But we are asked to believe. And as a guide to our belief, we have the example of one whose sad dragging of His feet through the streets of Jerusalem was replaced by the ecstatic dance of the Resurrection. We have the example of the one whose dark, blood-stained garments were replaced by the brightness of glory.

Far-fetched? Perhaps. Real? Most definitely, if we allow ourselves to join in His dance.

❧16❧

O the idea was childish, but divinely beautiful.

JOHANN CHRISTOPH FRIEDRICH VON SCHILLER

One summer's day when taking my dog on a walk, I encountered some children climbing trees. I smiled at how much fun they were having, remembering how delightful it was for me to do the same thing when I was their age: above it all, surrounded by the leafy familiarity of my favorite tree, not a care in the world.

Upon returning home I noticed, two yards over, a tree that would have been the perfect climbing tree if I were still a child, still involved in that sort of endeavor. And before I knew it, I was involved in that sort of endeavor. People might have thought I was crazy, but I didn't care. There is something divinely beautiful about the childish, and I think we need to tap into that every now and then.

❧ 17 ❧

Not Truth, but Faith it is
That keeps the world alive.
EDNA ST. VINCENT MILLAY

We have faith that the sun will rise tomorrow. We have faith that the just are eventually rewarded and the bad get theirs in the end. We have faith that God is somehow mysteriously active in the world. We have faith that the world can still be a good place. We have faith that next year—maybe, just maybe—the Cubs could win a pennant. We have faith that our friends will be there for us. If we truly sit down and reflect on what faith we put in ourselves, in others, in our world, we'll usually find that we have more faith than we might see at first glance. If we can have so much faith at so many times in our lives, we should have faith in the more difficult times of our lives. And truly this faith can keep us—and our world—alive.

❧ 18 ❧

You received without payment, give without payment.
MATTHEW 10:8

I inherited my love of books from my mother. I inherited my love of storytelling from my grandfather. I inherited my love of receiving mushy affection from my grandmother. And so it is that every time I write something or share something I'm reading with a friend; every time I tell a story, trying to achieve that same twinkle in my brown eyes that was clearly present in Gramps' blue eyes; every time I am unafraid to let down my guard and show unbridled affection for someone I love—a part of my mother, my grandfather and my grandmother lives on in me. And at those moments they don't seem so far away.

❧ 19 ❧

Creativity is more important than knowledge.

ALBERT EINSTEIN

When I was in kindergarten I made a necklace for my mother out of paper clips covered in orange-and-brown-patterned contact paper. I realize now, of course, that it was hideous, but at the time I thought it quite beautiful and was inordinately proud of it. My sense of pride exploded within me when, getting ready for a party one evening, she chose the necklace as the perfect compliment for her evening wear.

We spend a great deal of time trying to know what it is we need to know: how to do our work, how to deal with others, how to get beyond things in life that are weighing us down. But somewhere in the midst of all of our knowledge we also must realize that the sheer wonder of creating something—a painting, a poem—can bring much more beauty (and perspective) into our lives than a thousand textbooks can.

❧ 20 ❧

He said not, "Thou shall not be tempested, thou shall not be travailed, thou shall not be diseased;" but he said, "Thou shall not be overcome."

JULIAN OF NORWICH

"I never promised you a rose garden," the popular song goes, and most of us agree. Jesus makes it pretty clear what He promises those who will follow Him: hardship, trial, persecution. We feel sometimes that what we get is not the rose, but the thorn. And so we struggle, trying to make sense of it all, trying to keep our head above ground as we seek to grow in spite of some severe pruning.

We need never lose sight of another of the Lord's promises: I will be with you until the end of time. Life, for all its thorns and brambles, cannot completely bury us for He is with us. And even after the day when life finally does bury us, we know that He is still with us, as the thorns of this life give way to the most beautiful rose of eternity.

❧ 21 ❧

What in me is dark Illumine,
what is low raise and support.

JOHN MILTON

It's a simple prayer and one that can easily find voice on our lips. There are those places within us, shaded by fear, darkened by grief, tinted by confusion, that long to be enlightened, but we do not always know how to allow the light to pierce the darkness. There are those times in our lives when we feel low, burdened with sorrow, nearly crushed with grief, and we long to be raised above it all.

And so we pray to be enlightened, to be lifted up. And it can seem at times that God stands monstrously silent, but it is a silence that asks us to look not listen: to look at a man burdened with a cross, lifted up, who has become the very light of the world. It won't always make us feel better, this answer, but it is the only answer we've got.

❧ 22 ❧

Bless the Lord, frosts and snows
Sing praise to him and highly exalt him forever.

DANIEL 3:71

The spring weather had been pleasant, mild and sunny. Not only the early-risers such as the daffodils decided to emerge from the winter's sleep, but the more cautious tulips had made their appearance as well. All around were the enchanting colors of the season—the greens just a little more green; the yellows and reds just a little more so.

And then it happened: the frost. A killing frost that came in the midst of this loveliness to announce that winter was not so far removed. And many of us resented it, this frost—resented its ugly arrival on a scene that had been all too beautiful. Begrudgingly we had to admit: This frost somehow came from God, and was so connected to the beauty that there couldn't quite be a real recognition of one without the other.

❧ 23 ❧

The Israelites wept, "If only we had meat to eat!...
But now our strength is dried up
and there is nothing at all but this manna to look at."

NUMBERS 11:4-6

First they were in slavery in Egypt and the Lord led them out, going so far as to part the sea to get them to safety. Then they were hungry, and the Lord rained down manna from Heaven for them so that all they had to do was pick it up in the morning and eat. Then, even the manna wasn't enough; they wanted meat. It all smacks just a bit of ingratitude. But then they had been through a great deal and they still weren't where they ultimately wanted to be, and gratitude isn't always easy when you're in a place you don't want to be.

This same patience should be extended to us when we find that we are weary from the journey and have yet to reach our destination. Perhaps a little grumbling is fine as long as we remember that we, in the manner of this original group of grumblers, will also reach our destination.

❧ 24 ❧

But I have promises to keep,
And miles to go before I sleep,
And miles to go before I sleep.

ROBERT FROST

"How can I go on?" she asked me, standing at the open casket of her husband of 37 years. I wanted to answer, but wasn't sure the time was right to tell her. "You'll go on," I wanted to say, "because the human spirit has an amazing resiliency. You'll go on because you're stubborn. You'll go on because the alternative just won't do. You'll go on because even if life seems horrid and frightening and unfair and wretched right now you know that, in addition to all those things, it can be not-half-bad as well." I wanted to say it all, but instead I just said, "I don't know, I don't know," and held her hand. She seemed to think it was a good enough answer at the time.

❦ 25 ❦

Remember, man, that you are dust, and unto dust you shall return.

FORMULA FOR THE DISTRIBUTION OF ASHES,
ASH WEDNESDAY

On Ash Wednesday, as Christians come forward in church to receive the sign of ashes on their foreheads, thus beginning the penitential season of Lent, most thoughts are turned to sorrow for sin and firm amends to try and live better lives. Another formula—"Turn away from sin and be faithful to the Gospel"—ties in with this, and, perhaps because these particular words seem so fitting, this is the option that seems most often used.

I like the dust imagery better. Because in recognizing that we too shall some day turn to dust, we are keeping the precious, limited nature of life before our eyes—always a good thing. But also, foreheads smudged, we are mindful of those who have already gone before us and just how like them, and connected to them, we are.

❦ 26 ❦

Everywhere, we learn only from those whom we love.

GOETHE

How nice it would be if, when mourning, when questioning why, when giving in to anger, we could turn to a book that would help us put things in perspective, help us make sense of it all, help us to know unequivocally why things in our life went the way they did.

The Bible helps us do this—the Bible, and the people we love.

❧ 27 ❧

All work and no play makes Jack a dull boy.

JAMES HOWELL

This is one of those lines that has been around for a while, but I was never sure how long. Surely it is a modern quote, as only we post-industrial moderns allow work to rule our lives, right? Wrong. The words were written in 1659, showing that our desire to keep busy—often to a fault—is something that apparently we have been about for some time.

We work for so many reasons. To get ahead; to be able to afford things for our family and children; to assure ourselves security down the road; to somehow express who we are.

But if we work to forget or escape, then perhaps we should reflect on what it is we want to forget or escape and sharpen our ability to cope by relying on God, family and friendship.

❧ 28 ❧

Bliss in possession will not last;
Remembered joys are never past.

JAMES MONTGOMERY

One of my favorite pictures from our family album shows my parents and my father's cousin and her husband mugging for the camera with goofy, hysterical faces. My mother in her robe looks frail, a testimony to the fact that it was obviously taken at a time when happiness was probably in short supply. So much in the picture is no longer around; we've lived in several different houses since; we have new furniture, new drapes, new lamps; my father's cousin is no longer married to the man in the picture; my mother is no longer alive. But for all the transitory things that are there in that faded Polaroid, the sheer joy of the moment will never die.

❧ 29 ❧

Rock of Ages, cleft for me,
Let me hide myself in thee.

AUGUSTUS MONTAGUE TOPLADY

When I was young and would have bad dreams, I would cover my head completely under the covers, thinking that the monsters of childhood couldn't hurt me if they couldn't see me. On occasion though that wouldn't work, and I would rush out of bed into my parents' room. If the occasional monster could somehow penetrate my covers, it most certainly couldn't penetrate those of my parents. I would rest peacefully there until I awoke the next day, mysteriously back in my own bed.

The monsters of the adult world—regret, fear, loss, anxiety—aren't so easily vanquished. But if we realize that we still can hide ourselves in the loving familiarity of our God then we may find the monsters don't have the final say, and peaceful rest can be ours.

If we realize that we can still hide ourselves
in the loving familiarity of our God
then we may find the monsters don't have the final say,
and peaceful rest can be ours.

❧ 30 ❧

Now is the acceptable time! Now is the day of salvation!

2 C O R I N T H I A N S 6:2

All too often, in order to understand our suffering a little better, we look to the future: "I know that this is going to make me stronger someday, I just have to hold out until then." In all of this, we keep our eyes and hearts firmly planted on a day in the future, when the pain will be gone and in its place strength will be ours.

It is important for us to realize that although it might be natural to wish for a day when the pain will be gone, we must never lose sight that now, in this moment we wish were over, God's grace is powerfully present. To paraphrase that other Lewis writer, C.S., the pain we experience now and the beauty of that future moment are connected; the beauty then is a part of the pain now, and vice versa. And seeing this, not wishing it away, is the real grace of suffering.

MAY

🎐 1 🎐

Let the same mind be in you that was in Christ Jesus.

PHILIPPIANS 2:5

We can be stubborn. We can hold to our own thoughts and our own way of doing things with dogged tenacity, as if we have all the answers, as if no one else knows quite as much as we do. We can firmly plant our feet where we are, refusing to move forward, refusing to heed the voices of those who may call us forward. We can hold our own self-will as the model for how we—and a great part of the world—should react. We can do all of this, and at one time or another we probably have.

Or we can have Christ's attitude, who realized that His will had to also be the will of the Father; who knew that to really be filled He had to empty Himself; who knew that to really live He had to die; who knew that to really be exalted He had to be brought low.

Our attitude seems so much easier but is ultimately less successful.

🎐 2 🎐

If you continue in my word, you are truly my disciples;
and you will know the truth, and the truth will make you free.

JOHN 8:31-32

"Truth hurts!" I remember hearing kids yell on the playground to punctuate a nasty comment. And truly there can be something painful about truth which can slap us in the face even when we would rather not know the real story; which can lay bare all white lies, making them appear not-so-white after all. Yes, truth can indeed hurt.

That's why Jesus' offer of the truth, with the added promise that we will somehow be set free by it, can be a bit jarring for those of us who have said, from time to time, "What they don't know won't hurt them." Indeed, Jesus seems to be saying, what we don't know can indeed hurt us, and then, even after we know, the truth can continue to hurt us. Of course, as is the case with Jesus, His pain brings healing and promise.

❧ 3 ❧

It is a wonderful seasoning of all enjoyments
to think of those we love.

MOLIÈRE

I was one of those children who actually liked going to school. But now and then, when May would roll around and the robins would taunt me on the sun-drenched lawn outside, the day became a drudgery, something odious to be endured. And so I would look out the window and think of going home, of being with the neighborhood gang and getting into some kind of mischief, of being with my family and sharing a meal and a laugh.

In addition to being an antidote for a bad day, thinking of the ones we love can also help make a wonderful day all the more wonderful. And so every time I encounter something new and delightful I think of my family, my friends, and even those people who are no longer with me in this life. And in sharing my happiness with them, I am connected to them.

❧ 4 ❧

For the measure you give will be the measure you get back.

LUKE 6:36-38

Of all the measurable commodities perhaps none is so precious as time. There are only so many hours in the day, and there are so many things we feel we need to do, that making it happen seems daunting—if not downright impossible. And so we can feel we just have no time to write a note to someone we know is suffering or pay a visit to someone who really needs support or even pick up the phone to bolster the drooping spirits of another.

If we don't make time for these people, however, we might find that others won't make time for us when we suffer, when we need support, when our spirits droop. Time, as precious as it is, demands to be shared with others—not hoarded.

❧ 5 ❧

"Tut, tut, child," said the Duchess.
"Everything's got a moral if only you can find it."

LEWIS CARROLL

Some say everything you need to know you learn in kindergarten. I myself think this is ridiculous because I, for one, never heard anything about the internet or tax breaks—for instance—in kindergarten. I would be much more comfortable modifying the statement to: Everything you need to know you learn in life. And how true this is. Through the death of my mother I learned how precious life is; through my own illness I learned to appreciate health; through confusion and doubt I learned to believe.

I guess it would be nice if all of our lessons could be like kindergarten—complete with snack time, a nap and story time. But it is ultimately more rewarding, I think, to find the moral in life by living out the story, not just hearing about it.

❧ 6 ❧

Batter my heart, three-person'd God; for you
As yet but knock, breathe, shine, and seek to mend.

JOHN DONNE

It may not always be pleasant the way God knocks on our hearts or batters us with His persistent Spirit until we acquiesce and let Him in. God's knocking can take so many different forms—even the sorrow of loss. For in our longing to be with someone we are giving voice to that ultimate longing wherein we long to be united with God. It's hard to see this though, when our hearts are battered. But infinitely easier when they are mended, which can only happen when we acknowledge the One at the door.

❧ 7 ❧

He who created you without you will justify you without you.

AUGUSTINE OF HIPPO

"I'm angry with You, God," I said, "and I want nothing to do with You."
"Oh, but I am everything to do with you," said God. "I hurt, God," I
said, "and You seem to be the cause." "Oh, but in your pain is my love,"
said God. "I am confused, God, and You seem nothing but a mystery
with no chance of solving." "Oh, but in the mystery is the answer to
everything," said God. "I miss them, O God, and You apparently took
them from me." "Oh, but in the emptiness of your heart you can still
have them," said God.

"I can't seem to get away from You, God," I said. "Oh, but you're
right," said God. And love was the language of it all.

❧ 8 ❧

Strike the rock, and the water will come out of it,
so that the people may drink.

EXODUS 17:6

One of my favorite stories is "The Selfish Giant" by Oscar Wilde,
wherein a nasty, selfish giant's stony heart is touched by the love of a
special child and his life here (and in the hereafter) is changed forever.
The moral of the story is that Christ can make love spring forth from
even the hardest of hearts.

We need to believe that. We need to believe that even if our hearts
seem rock-hard, the awareness of Christ can change our hearts, bringing
solace where there was sorrow, forgiveness where there was resentment,
peace where there was turmoil. Hearts of stone thus pierced, we can
help soften the hearts of others with the beautiful, refreshing grace that
had been flooded over us.

❧ 9 ❧

Reading is to the mind what exercise is to the body.

JOSEPH ADDISON

The first book I remember reading was *The Wind in the Willows* by Kenneth Grahame. It is a wonderful book, filled with joy and treachery and love and envy and, in the end, peace. I remember slowly making my way through the book with my mother, enthralled by the discovery that letters on a page could combine to reach into my soul and give voice to the joy and treachery and love and envy and peace that I experienced in my own life.

Good writers tell stories in ways that, even though the story is uniquely theirs, we can nevertheless see ourselves in. And so what a worthwhile exercise it is to open a book in our constant attempt to understand the stories of our lives.

❧ 10 ❧

When the people set out from their tents to cross over the Jordan, the priests bearing the ark of the covenant were in front of the people.

JOSHUA 3:14

It had been a long journey, beginning with slavery in Egypt before deliverance from Pharaoh's bonds, to the vast expansiveness of the wilderness. It was filled with confusion and doubt. They wondered what exactly their God had gotten them into. And yet they heard over and over for a generation that He would deliver them, and so they marched on and came to this point where they crossed the Jordan and finally entered into that land which had been promised them so long ago.

Even in the midst of some backsliding they stuck with their God, and He delivered them. He will do the same for us.

❧ 11 ❧

Then they told what had happened on the road, and how he had
been made known to them in the breaking of the bread.

LUKE 24:35

On a lonesome, dusty road some saddened men encounter a stranger.
They tell Him the story of their sadness, how they had put their hope
in this Jesus and He had been executed like a common criminal. And
now friends were saying that His tomb was empty, causing all kinds
of confusion. The stranger talks to them, to try to help them put their
world back in order. And in the midst of these ordinary men with
ordinary woes the stranger breaks ordinary bread and suddenly they
realize that what appears ordinary is not ordinary at all—but Jesus
Himself breaking through with His extraordinary presence.

It is important to pay attention to the ordinary, because one never
knows what might come of it.

❧ 12 ❧

He told me everything I have ever done.

JOHN 4:39

It can be unnerving thinking of an all-knowing, all-present, all-seeing
God. Those of us who were raised on the American ideals of freedom
and individuality just might balk at the image of a God who is always
watching us like Orwell's Big Brother. It can seem a bit invasive.

Or comforting. Because what a solace it can be to think that God
knows all our struggles, our sufferings, our confusion, our fear. What
a relief to know that even if we battle something over and over again,
God is there for every battle and knows what a toll other such battles
have taken on us. If we survived them, it was due in large part to this
all-knowing, all-present, all-seeing God, passionately in love with us,
intimately involved. Knowing how we survived then will help us survive
the same things in the future.

❧13❧

Fading, fading; strength beyond hope and despair…

T. S. ELIOT

Not long after his father died my friend James was in the grocery store, in that strange place where the extraordinary peculiarity of the loss of a loved one exists side by side with the routine of everyday life. His father's unexpected death had been just one more in a series of crushing blows, and his very faith was shaken to its core. Maybe years of prayer and trying to live the Christian life just weren't worth it, he found himself thinking.

"Paper or plastic?" the check-out girl asked, the mundane question jolting him temporarily out of his deep despair. He looked up to answer, and saw that her name tag said, "Hope." And he did.

❧14❧

God is love.

1 JOHN 4:8

During a morality class in college, the professor turned the discussion to love. We had at this point studied all kinds of philosophical definitions of love. We spent what seemed like weeks on the writings of Augustine. And so wanting, I suppose, a synthesis of what we had learned to that point, he asked the class, "What is love?" Then he called on James.

James opened his mouth and sputtered and stuttered so much that it almost sounded like a groan. The professor moved on to someone else, who answered the question more to his liking.

I can't help but think, however, that James' answer hit closer to the mark. If God is love, then love is eternal, loving, all-knowing and not just a little bit confusing.

❧15❧

Where'er we tread 'tis haunted, holy ground.

GEORGE NOEL GORDON, LORD BYRON

After the death of Joseph Cardinal Bernardin, my friends David and Stephanie and I decided to drive three and a half hours to pay our respects to this man who had meant so much to us in different ways. And so we began our journey to Chicago, a journey that we had made countless times before for Cubs games, Bulls games, weekend getaways and social engagements.

This time, the road was different. Boring Interstate 57 suddenly seemed a beautiful road made significant by our pilgrimage.

We sometimes tend to limit holiness to churches or grand, lush scenes. But any path upon which we walk—any path which leads us to significant moments of grace and insight—has the ability to be an avenue of holiness if we pay attention to the journey.

❧16❧

Who would have thought my shrivel'd heart
Could have recovered greenness?

GEORGE HERBERT

My mother died in the summer at a time when a young boy's thoughts should be turned to games of baseball and hide-and-seek. A few days after the funeral, life once again returned to a semblance of routine: Dad worked, we went to church, but I couldn't bring myself to go out and play, even though the very nature of summer seemed to demand it. No, I would never play again, I was determined. My young heart was so cold it might as well have been winter.

But slowly the rays of the sun enticed me through the windows and I ventured outside. And breathing in the exciting possibilities of a summer day, I found my way to my neighbor's house to see if maybe something was going on. My life would never be the same, I knew, but it could be good again. And so I ran to get my bicycle.

❧ 17 ❧

I will look to the Lord, I will wait for the God of my salvation.
MICAH 7:7

It can seem as if God doesn't always care. It can seem as if we have to bear our sorrow alone. It can seem as if God doesn't listen to our prayers. And when it seems this way, we need to pray for the grace to realize that the sunrise each morning, bathing us in light, is a sign that God cares; a smile brushing ever-so-briefly across our lips is a sign that God sends joy into our lives; the feeling, however fleeting, that the people we love are somehow encouraged and protected by that love is a sign that our prayers are indeed heard.

Life goes much smoother and seems to make more sense if we look to the Lord—and His signs—first, before anything else.

❧ 18 ❧

The earth, and every common sight,
To me did seem
Appareled in celestial light.
WILLIAM WORDSWORTH

When I was in junior high school, I spent a lot of time on the phone. Perhaps my favorite conversations were with my friend Stephanie who lived across the street. If I used the phone at my father's desk and she used the phone in her living room, we could sit in our respective windows and look at one another while we talked. That we could have easily hung up, gone out our front doors, and spoken in person didn't seem to be as fun; perhaps what made it more interesting was that we were able to see one another using a manner of communication that ordinarily involved only talking and listening.

So often in prayer we try to communicate with a God we cannot see. Perhaps if we also reflect on the God we can see—the face of a cherished friend, a painted sky at sunset—prayer might be all the more interesting.

❧ 19 ❧

Now the whole group of those who believed
were of one mind and one heart.

ACTS OF THE APOSTLES 4:32

How was it that a frightened, mostly uneducated group of people in a remote part of the world two thousand years ago could pass along a message that has not only survived all this time but has gone on to change the world and the scope of human history? How was it that the Early Church survived horrific setbacks, oppression and persecution? Through the Spirit, of course, but specifically through the Spirit binding them together in love so that they realized they were in it all together.

When we find ourselves saying, "I can do this on my own," we very obviously haven't learned the power of being of one mind and heart with a community of believers.

❧ 20 ❧

When you have nothing to say, say nothing.

CHARLES CALEB COLTON

Perhaps one of the biggest misconceptions about prayer is that if we're not doing or saying something we're not really praying. And so we go about the task of memorizing formulae, of ticking off our prayer lists to God as if we are strolling down an aisle of the grocery store, afraid we'll forget the coffee filters or laundry detergent.

But prayer also occurs when we just don't have anything to say, when the dynamics of life are so confusing that words would only muddy life's waters even more. We need to realize that just because we can't bring ourselves to say anything to God in prayer doesn't mean that communication with Him is not there. God's communication with us is like His love for us—eternal—and so silence is not necessarily merely a lack of sound but a continuation of the conversation that was begun before the ages.

❦ 21 ❦

He cried out in a loud voice, "Lazarus, come out!" The dead man came out, his hands and feet bound with strips of cloth, his face wrapped in a cloth. Jesus said to them, "Unbind him, and let him go."

JOHN 11:43-44

It was long ago, this story of Lazarus with its stifling heat, its oppressive grief, and its miraculous ending. And there is a sense in which we can't relate to the story, we who unlike Martha and Mary have had to suffer loss without our dead walking back into life. But if we only view the story from the perspective of the mourners, we're missing an important point: How like Lazarus we all are. Who among us has not felt dead, shut away in darkness, fettered by the strands of sorrow? And the same Lord comes to us, enters into our stifling heat, our oppressive grief, and offers us a miraculous ending: Come out!

Lazarus learned what we too should know: It is only through encounters with this Jesus that we can be truly free of those things that keep us tied down.

❦ 22 ❦

And Stephen's face was like the face of an angel.

ACTS OF THE APOSTLES 6:15

He endured the angry words of the crowd screaming at him to stop preaching of this man named Jesus. He endured imprisonment and was put behind bars for believing that Jesus had risen from the dead. And ultimately he endured death, raising his eyes to Heaven and praying for those who would take his life even as the stones began to assault him. And through all of this, Stephen's face seemed like that of an angel. How was it that he could be so serene, so confident, when fear and violence surrounded him? It is very difficult for us to understand, we who can fret and worry about so very little.

Stephen's strength, of course, came from the fact that he never took his eyes off the Lord Jesus. How easier our lives would be if we looked in that same direction.

❧ 23 ❧

All experience is an arch, to build upon.

HENRY BROOKS ADAMS

My mother taught me how to read, an obvious expression of her love for me. My father taught me to be good to others and to myself, an obvious expression of his love for me. My stepmother taught me to stick with things, even when they didn't go the way I would have liked them to go, an obvious expression of her love for me. And on and on goes the list of people who have taught me because they loved me.

Of course I cannot deny that I have learned much through the death of my mother and my grandparents, my sister's battle with cancer, as well as my own battle. And I know that all of these experiences taught me so much and are an obvious expression of God's love for me. It's just that I don't always understand this kind of love and so I resist it.

❧ 24 ❧

Nothing in the world is single,
All things by a law divine
In one spirit meet and mingle.

PERCY BYSSHE SHELLEY

A cardinal rule of pastoral counseling is to never allow yourself to fall into the trap of saying, "I know how you feel." The way people grieve and the circumstances of loss are as different as people are different. Just because I lost my mother as a young boy, for example, doesn't mean that I presume to know how all young boys who lose their mothers feel.

That being said, there is an element of grief that is common to everyone: To suffer is to be human. Every time we feel some sort of suffering or grief in our lives it is connected somehow to everyone who suffers, everyone who grieves. And though these nameless, faceless people don't know exactly how we feel, we are connected through a law divine—one Spirit.

❦ 25 ❦

Uphold me, O God, according to your promise, and I shall live;
and do not confound me in my expectation.

FROM THE RITE OF MONASTIC PROFESSION (PSALM 118)

During the presidential election of 1976, President Ford's train was scheduled to make a stop in our small town, population 2,500. The day arrived and the preparations were complete. Banners were made, businesses closed, the high school band was present to greet him. The train was seen in the distance, a cry was heard, and as the train drew closer the band struck up their song while people waved their banners. The president's train slowed down, but just that—it didn't stop, having, we learned later, fallen too far behind schedule. The crowd stood stunned as the train pulled away. The disappointment was palpable, the dashing of expectations actualized by the crashing of cymbals.

Life can offer one disappointment after another, but God will always uphold us. He has promised.

❦ 26 ❦

I have come as light into the world, so that everyone
who believes in me should not remain in darkness.

JOHN 12:46

The scene is always the same: a darkened sky, perhaps with streaks of deep red running through it; blustering wind; and three crosses rising up from barren, rocky ground. It is a tragic scene, and the darkness that surrounds it is a link to so much that can frighten us—the darkness under the bed, the darkness of the closet, the darkness of being lost.

And yet somehow, eventually, the darkness is replaced by a sky streaked by brilliant colors of light, fertile ground, and white garments. And the oppressive fear of the darkness gives way to light, bathing everyone and everything in its path with life, hope, love.

This scene is not just played out in the pages of Scripture and on movie screens. It is played out in the very story of humanity, and its life, hope and promise, is offered freely to us. We need only believe.

❦ 27 ❦

Jesus said to his disciples, "Do not let your hearts be troubled."
JOHN 14:1

We all face a legion of worries, often on a daily basis. Basic questions of family struggles, financial concerns and work pressures combine with issues of anger, sadness, loss and confusion. When this occurs, our lives, our thoughts, our hearts can be filled with the constant awareness of the struggle, a constant awareness that life's journey can be arduous, not always easy to manage.

And in the midst of all this Jesus tells us not to let our hearts be worried. Is He crazy? Could He really be saying this if He walked in our shoes for a bit? Of course, He did walk in our shoes, and as crazy as it may sound we can have hearts free from trouble if we trust in His presence, if we believe that, as He changed water into wine, He can change us as well.

❦ 28 ❦

I have a song to sing, O! Sing me your song, O!
SIR WILLIAM SCHWENCK GILBERT

I love to tell stories, to talk about things that have happened to me that touched me, things that have shaped me, given me insight that just begs for me to share it. I don't tell stories because it's an entertaining thing to do, although it is. I don't tell stories because it's a wonderful way to educate, although it is. I tell stories so that somewhere in my experiences, others may see glimpses of their own experiences, and the memories which can turn into grace in my life may see the same transformation in the lives of those listening. And so it is important for us to tell our stories—both happy and sad. Not only that, but it is vital that we listen to one another's stories as well. In this exchange, this communication, we get an idea of how connected we all are.

❧29❧

Save yourselves from this corrupt generation.

ACTS OF THE APOSTLES 2:40

There has been in the history of monasticism an "us and them" mentality: Monks flee the world and all its wicked ways while others live in the midst of the wickedness. And when carried to the extreme, we view the world as inherently bad and the safety of the cloister as more sacred. This mentality is harmful because it doesn't take into consideration all the wonderful things God can and does do even in the midst of a crooked world.

This is not to say, however, that all of us, whether we're monks or not, should not resist "the world." The world can sometimes promote each man for himself, but we know the way of God is to care for one another. The world can tell us that we need to get over it and move on, but we know life is a long journey, a slow process.

The world can tell us
that we need to get over it and move on,
but we know life is a long journey, a slow process.

✣ 30 ✣

Strive for the greater gifts.

1 CORINTHIANS 12:31

Not being married myself, it has been a real blessing for me to be able to spend time with my friends Marty and Liz. Whether it's looking at their boys' homework or eating pizza and watching movies, their love for one another and their family spills out and envelopes me as well, mirroring God's love, which is what marriage is supposed to be about. What a gift!

I have also been around them, however, in times of struggle, harsh words and doubt. And although Marty and Liz might not see it, these times too are somehow a gift. It's just that we often think in our short-sightedness that gifts are only those things that make us feel good. We can sometimes wish to ignore the Cross, which is far from pleasant but is nevertheless God's love spilling out and enveloping us. What a gift!

✣ 31 ✣

The ripest peach is highest on the tree.

JAMES WHITCOMB RILEY

We are all inspired at one time or another by stories of little people overcoming enormous obstacles to achieve greatness. These people are able to achieve because they keep their eyes and hearts firmly planted on the goal in front of them; they will allow nothing that life throws at them to get in the way of their dream. And we are inspired by this because we know just how high the hurdles of life can be that litter our path.

Learning lessons from these people, we begin to realize that keeping our eyes on the goal is the key. "How am I going to get through this?" we may ask ourselves, looking at each obstacle as insurmountable. But if we can pray for the strength to see the end beyond the obstacles, odds are good that we too can attain what it is we seek, that ripest peach.

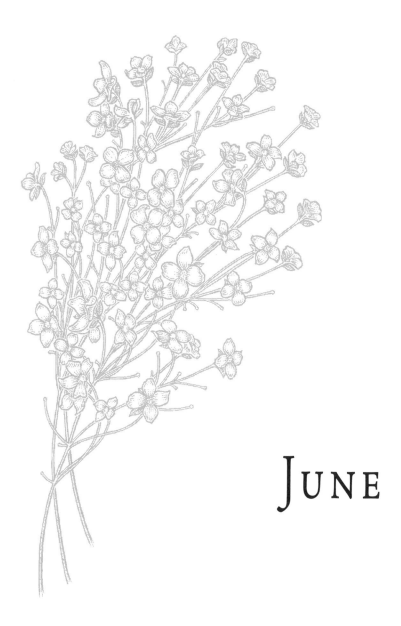

JUNE

✵ 1 ✵

Nothing is so useless as a general maxim.

JULIA CRAWFORD

After the death of my mother, I heard many well-intentioned people say so many of the same things to me: Be strong, your mother would have wanted it that way; You should be thankful that she is not suffering anymore; I know how you feel, I lost my mother too. And, although I knew they meant well, I wanted to scream at them: "Maybe my mother would have wanted me to cry and carry on, how do you know?" While I was thankful she wass not suffering, I couldn't quite get around the fact that I was suffering, too.

It might be a comfort to know that other people have suffered tragedy and loss in their lives and moved on. But it is also a comfort to know that no one has experienced it quite like we have.

✵ 2 ✵

Your steadfast love, O Lord, extends to the heavens,
your faithfulness to the clouds.

PSALM 36

I love to lie in the sun. I know that it is bad for me, but feeling the warmth of the sun's rays on my body is one of the nicest sensations going, if you ask me. Perhaps even more wonderful than that though is the feeling that comes about merely staring up at the limitless expanse of the sky. When it seems as if the pressure, struggle and sadness of the world can crowd me in, taking a few minutes to look upward makes me aware of how small some of my problems are compared with the love of a God who fills all the blue space above.

❦ 3 ❦

Go into all the world
and proclaim the good news to the whole creation.

MARK 16:15

Peter and John could have offered all kinds of excuses as to why they couldn't perform the tasks they were chosen to perform. How can I preach when I can barely read? How can I offer keen theological insights when I have never formally studied? How can I make a lame man walk when I know nothing about the healing arts? All kinds of excuses could have been made, but in the end Peter and John knew that the key was not how educated or high-born or even how qualified they were to do what the Lord had asked of them. No, the key was their faith that God could work amazing things through them, through their weakness, through their frail humanity with all its limitations.

"How can I get through this?" we are tempted to ask ourselves from time to time. Peter and John clearly knew the answer. Do we?

❦ 4 ❦

The apostles and the elders met together to consider this matter.

ACTS OF THE APOSTLES 15:6

There can be a tendency to romanticize the Early Church at times, to wonder why things and people can't be as faith-filled as things and people were in the first centuries after the death and resurrection of Jesus. Indeed, there is much we can learn from the heroic faith of these ancestors of ours.

It is also important to remember, however, that in addition to the wondrous, almost idyllic faith that was evidenced among these people, they also had to deal with dissension, controversy, confusion and sorrow. Perhaps the real thing that separates us from them is that they knew they could not deal with it all alone but rather relied on one another to help make sense of it.

It would behoove us to follow their lead, convening and looking into the matter.

❧ 5 ❧

One ought, every day at least, to hear a little song,
read a good poem, see a fine picture,
and, if it were possible to speak a few reasonable words.

GOETHE

My first exposure to poetry (outside of nursery rhymes) was reading Vachel Lyndsay's "The Congo" with my mother. The poem has a nice musicality about it with a refrain that calls to mind tribal drums beating deep in the heart of the African jungle. What a world it opened up to me, this curious poem. What a delight it was learning the words of it myself, sharing in the drama of it, shouting out "Boomlay boomlay boomlay boom!" and then collapsing into my mother, giggling from the excitement of it all.

That there is something about poetry and literature and art and music that taps into a unique part of the human soul is beyond doubt. But I have also discovered, especially every time I now read this old familiar poem, that perhaps it can tap into the souls of those who have gone before us as well.

*I have also discovered that perhaps poetry can tap
into the souls of those who have gone before us as well.*

❧ 6 ❧

Old and young, we are all on our last cruise.

ROBERT LOUIS STEVENSON

Saint Benedict encourages monks to keep death daily before our eyes. This is perhaps best demonstrated when a monk professes solemn vows for life. The monk lies prostrate on the floor and is covered with a funeral pall. The bell ordinarily reserved for announcing the death of a monk is tolled. The cantor intones an antiphon that begins: "Now I am dead." This can all seem a bit morbid to people, and it has been known to startle visitors.

But the truth of it all remains, even if we don't like to think about it: All of us will die. And realizing this somehow makes us live better, if we pay attention to life. It also makes those who have gone before us in death not seem so remote from us, for we realize that they have gone where we will one day follow.

❧ 7 ❧

What passion cannot music rise and quell?

JOHN DRYDEN

One of my favorite stories as a child was *The Secret Garden*, by Frances Hodges Burnett. In the story, a bitter young girl's life is transformed through the wonders of a garden. Not too long ago, I saw a musical version of the tale and it only added to the beauty of it. There is perhaps no better vehicle for a story than through the wonders of music.

Even if we can't sing a note, even if we don't know Mozart from Madonna, there exists within music—from Bach to the Backstreet Boys—something that can touch us in a way that nothing or no one else can. No one, of course, but God, whose ultimate symphony of love is the fullest expression of every note ever written.

✿ 8 ✿

There is no substitute for hard work.

THOMAS ALVA EDISON

Work. For some the word calls to mind careers, whatever allows us to acquire the things in life that we need. For some the word calls to mind a different kind of labor: working in the garden, cleaning the house, whatever it is that allows us to get done the things that need to get done to make our surroundings more pleasing, more bearable.

Life, of course, is work, although we don't always want to think of it that way. But if we are to acquire that which we really need (love, security, hope) and if we are able to make our surroundings more pleasing, more bearable (through forgiveness, healing, patience) then we must work at it. There really is no substitute.

✿ 9 ✿

There is more to life than increasing its speed.

MAHATMA GANDHI

Where's the fire? Haste makes waste. Slow and steady wins the race. What's your hurry? Our language is so filled with aphorisms and phrases (speedily uttered, of course) that it is not difficult to draw the conclusion that many of us have a difficult time slowing down. Maybe we have too much to do and we need to crowd as much as we can into a short span of time. Maybe the world itself revolves at a hectic pace and we need to move quickly just to keep up. Maybe we think if we speed from one thing to another we can outrun those things such as sorrow, regret and pain. We should take as our model of course the One whose slow descent through the streets of Jerusalem and slow ascent to the wood of the Cross has given the world the ultimate model of what life is really about.

❦10❦

I trusted in your steadfast love.

PSALM 13

I can remember thinking after my mother died that I wasn't quite sure whether I wanted to live in a world like the one I was in. I looked around and I saw three motherless children and a husband devoid of the presence of a wife. This tempered my vision so I started seeing tragedy and suffering everywhere and very little else. This was the world, and I quite frankly didn't want anything to do with it, although I knew that I would continue to have everything to do with it.

There are still times when I lament that the world is not what it should be. But I also see people being kind to one another, the beauty of nature, the wonders of loving relationships. And seeing these signs all around me I realize that the tragedies of the world do not have the final say to one who trusts in God's merciful love.

❦11❦

The beautiful souls are they that are universal,
open and ready for all things.

MONTAIGNE

The death of a loved one can birth a host of absolute statements: I'll never be truly happy again; I'll never marry again; I'll always feel alone in this world; I'll never understand why this had to happen; I'll never accept this. And while such absolutes are natural, the reality of the situation is that growth comes not in allowing absolutes to crowd our life but by allowing possibilities to open up our lives. The fact remains that even if we cannot imagine it now we may be happy again, we may marry again, we may not always feel so alone, we may accept it all.

Loss closes off so much in our lives, makes so much ugly. Only the grace of acknowledging that possibilities exist can open our souls and restore some of the beauty that was once there.

❧ 12 ❧

I like to walk about the beautiful things that adorn the world.

GEORGE SANTAYANA

Every evening, if the weather is pleasant enough, several of us take a walk after dinner. The purpose of the walk is never exercise—indeed some of us have been chastised because we walk too fast. No, the purpose of the walk is to share a word or two with our brothers and drink in the beauty of the rolling hills of southern Indiana. We never really have anywhere to go so the destination is unimportant. The journey, however, is.

It is just such a notion that is the foundation of pilgrimage, even the pilgrimage known as life itself. In worrying about getting from Point A to Point B, or completely bypassing Point A or Point B because we don't like the scenery, we lose sight of the importance of the trip, where much is discovered about ourselves, about others and about God.

❧ 13 ❧

Shared joy is double joy, and shared sorrow is half sorrow.

SWEDISH PROVERB

There are those who say you shouldn't complain about the hand that life has dealt you; no one likes a whiner—get over it. There are those who say if you are blessed with great fortune, you shouldn't advertise it; no one likes a braggart—keep it to yourself. People who say these things seem to miss the point. We are all connected on this planet and my joys and sorrows affect you just as your joys and sorrows affect me. We can no more make sense of the dreams and delights, the tragedies and terrors of life by ourselves than we can hope to simultaneously sing all the parts of Handel's *Messiah* alone.

❧14❧

I will be their God, and they shall be my people.

JEREMIAH 31:33

My grandmother made the best cinnamon rolls in the world. Soft bread, sticky cinnamon (especially in the middle), rich, thick icing: Eating one of these rolls was a connection to the best the world had to offer—sweetness, warmth, satisfaction.

I know now that the rolls were also a connection to Grandma, indeed to my entire family. Besides the amazing ingredients that went into them, Grandma put love and stories and life into them as well. Again and again I was able to taste this connection, to savor life's sweetness. And even though Grams is no longer here, every time I taste a bit of cinnamon, a bit of icing, I am able to have a little taste of her love, which was for me the best the world had to offer—sweetness, warmth, satisfaction.

❧15❧

Do not fear, only believe.

MARK 5:36

Once as a small boy, I remember being awakened in the middle of the night by a great deal of activity outside my bedroom door. My mother was sick, and an ambulance was there to take her to the hospital. Every night after this event I had terrible dreams, and I would wake up nearly paralyzed with fear, my very joints aching. Inevitably, I would make my way to my parents' room where my father would try to console me and put my fears to rest. My worrying was not going to make anything better, he would tell me. It wasn't the best explanation, but it worked at the time.

Many people face fear of one kind or another on a daily basis. In the midst of this Jesus tells us to replace our useless fear with trust. If we really do trust, if we really believe, it just might work.

❧ 16 ❧

Abide in my love.

JOHN 15:9

The resiliency of the human being is astounding. We live a life of constant change, of frequent struggle, of inestimable happiness. Indeed it is not uncommon for all these things to happen in our lives in relatively short periods of time. And through it all we somehow manage to move on, to keep trudging through a world that is fast-paced, wonderful and not just a little confusing.

How do we manage? What is it that enables us to take such a variety of experiences and make sense of them? What is it that enables us not to be done in by what can at times seem like the sheer enormity of a life lived to its fullest?

Some would say it's a mystery, and they're right, although perhaps not in the way that they think. It is a mystery. It is the mystery of God's passionate love for us.

❧ 17 ❧

Man needs to suffer. Griefs purify and prepare him.

JOSÉ MARTÍ

Anyone who regularly watches the evening news cannot fail but be mindful of the suffering in the world: natural disasters, violence, civil strife, hatred, immoral politicians—the list of the world's woes goes on and on. When you combine them with the personal woes that we and others experience, watching evening news can become like swallowing bitter medicine. We can begin to wonder if the price of being informed is worth the pain.

But every once in a while a story will come on about a family who lost everything but still managed to put their child through Harvard by selling handmade doormats. You realize that it is all worth it: The pain doesn't always have the final say.

❦ 18 ❦

This time, like all times, is a very good one,
if we but know what to do with it.

RALPH WALDO EMERSON

As children we learn to wish for the future: I wish I were old enough to stay up late; I wish I were sixteen so I could drive; I wish I were in college so that I could be on my own; I wish I had more seniority at work so that I could have more vacation time; I wish I was on vacation. And perhaps most deeply: I wish this hurt was over.

Wishing for a future removed from our present situation might be natural but it is clearly not the best thing. If we accept the grace that is around us we can learn so much from what is going on in our lives here and now and bring about a time when the hurt is really over.

❦ 19 ❦

A new heart I will give you, and a new spirit I will put within you;
and I will remove from your body the heart of stone
and give you a heart of flesh.

EZEKIEL 36:26

I once visited a woman in the hospital whose husband and son had perished in a fire that nearly claimed her own life. As soon as I walked into the room she screamed at me to leave. "I don't want anything to do with God!" she cried in anguish, her obvious pain causing me to wince. I left, and the nurses told me not to come back.

But I think about her often. Part of me wonders if her suffering did her in, if she is no longer able to live and love because of the tragedy of what she endured. You can't really blame her on one level for hardening her heart against God: It was all a bit too much.

Another part of me wonders—hopes—that a heart naturally hardened by such suffering could somehow be softened by a God who is also a bit too much.

❧ 20 ❧

Yes, Virginia, there is a Santa Claus.

FRANCIS PHARCELLUS CHURCH

It never dawned on me as a child how unlikely it all was, this Santa Claus business. That one man could somehow keep track of everyone who was naughty and everyone who was nice was astounding enough, but in addition to all of this he was somehow able to get to every single home in the world and deliver gifts in the span of a single night. Ignorance of the intricacies of intercontinental travel aside, one would have thought that I would have been able to figure it out, but I didn't. I wanted to believe, and the power of belief is a formidable entity.

Jesus promised that whoever believed in Him would never die. If I could believe in the myth of Santa Claus for so long, then how much more powerful should the effects of my belief in the very real words of Jesus be?

❧ 21 ❧

I will give you the keys of the kingdom of Heaven.

MATTHEW 16:19

Brother Methodius was an odd little man, or at least I remember him that way. A man of few words, he limped—shuffled really—around, whistling a tune I could never make out, keeping time by slapping his hand against the side of his leg. But for all his quirks, I once heard him described as the most powerful man here because being the locksmith he could open absolutely any door in this institution. There is definitely a power in possessing keys.

Imagine the power involved in being given the keys to the kingdom of Heaven. Although this power was given to Peter and his successors, we have a share in that power whenever we seek to open doors closed to sadness and struggle in order to see the promise that lies beyond. Imagine what life could be like if we opened such doors.

❦ 22 ❦

Love bade me welcome: yet my soul drew back,
Guilty of dust and sin.

GEORGE HERBERT

Peoples' notion of sin often falls into two opposing camps: Some people seem to see sin everywhere while others wouldn't know a sin (or at least acknowledge it) if it came up and bit them on the nose. The healthiest stance is in the middle somewhere, as the healthiest stance often is. We need to be patient with ourselves and others and realize that we are human and prone to fail from time to time. And yet we also must make sure that we acknowledge those times when we have consciously chosen something that we know is not right and hold ourselves accountable. In recognizing that which is mere human frailty as well as that which is just plain wrong, we begin to free ourselves from past hurts and fears and make room for Love.

❦ 23 ❦

Their eyes, mid many wrinkles, their eyes,
Their ancient, glittering eyes are gay.

WILLIAM BUTLER YEATS

She was always larger than life to me: big fleshy arms, hands that could squeeze my face so hard that I feared the indentations would be permanent; major laughing and crying—in both instances her dark eyes a troubadour of life's wonders. She had a nasty side (who doesn't) but I never saw it, only heard about it. Instead I experienced an enormous love that rushed out of her big heart, through her eyes to my eyes and rested in my heart.

As my grandmother lay dying, now small and frail, I was struck by the sense of loss of someone so grand to me, a loss that seemed to grow larger as her body grew smaller. But the last time I saw her, her eyes opened briefly and I caught just a glimpse of that big love. I realized it was still there somehow, being far too big to ever go away.

❧ 24 ❧

A leper came to [Jesus] begging him,
"If you choose, you can make me clean."
Moved with pity, Jesus stretched out his hand and touched him,
and said to him, "I do choose. Be made clean."

MARK 1:40-41

He wants the same for us. Aware of how we struggle, mindful of that within us which needs healing, moved with pity for us, He wants us to be cured as well. He desires not that sorrow and suffering should have the final say in our lives, but joy and life. He desires the darkness which can so surround us at times be vanquished by the inestimable brilliance of His light. He wills all of this for us, so great is His love.

We need only stretch out our hand to Him to be made clean.

❧ 25 ❧

One must not always think so much about what one should do,
but rather what one should be.

MEISTER ECKHART

"What do you do?" On a recent trip I encountered all kinds of adults who asked me that question. Part of the questioning I'm sure comes from a natural curiosity about monks—people worry that we sit and pray all day. But part of it comes from our society's emphasis on our individual worth stemming from what we do as our job: I pray; I write; I sing; I administrate.

In contrast to this is what children asked me: What's your favorite color? Do you like vegetables? Who's your favorite basketball player? The answers to these questions ultimately had more to do with who I am than those asked by their parents.

This is another example of how we should be childlike. God loves and helps us because of who we are, not what we do.

❧ 26 ❧

So they said to him, "What sign are you going to give us,
that we may see it and believe in you?"

JOHN 24:30

They had listened spellbound as he preached God's kingdom of love,
His words sounding like a beautiful symphony. They had seen Him
extend his hands in loving touch, bringing healing and solace to people
who needed His presence, His touch to go on living. They had seen
Him take five loaves and two fishes and from that feed thousands of
people. And still, after all this, they wanted a sign.

We're not too different from these people because we too long for
signs. And like these people the signs are in our midst: in the gentle fall
of spring rain, the anguished cry of a sorrowing mother, in the tender
caress of lovers. Yes, signs of God's care for us are all around us, but
all too often we are so preoccupied looking for the signs we think we
should see that we miss the ones in front of us.

❧ 27 ❧

And when he stepped out of the boat, immediately a man
out of the tombs with an unclean spirit met him.

MARK 5:2

Of all the people in need of Jesus' healing, perhaps none is as tragic as the
Gerasene demoniac, whose life was lived in darkness and desperation,
shackled to the harsh coldness of the tombs, bruising himself with
stones, crying out in anguish against demons that plagued him.

We, in perhaps different ways, face our demons too: demons of fear,
loss, regret, anger. And there are times when in despair we can allow
these demons to keep us shackled to fear, hurting ourselves with the
stones of regret, crying out in the anguish of loss. But if we accept the
healing touch of our God, so often manifested through caring people,
then we can begin to see the place of warmth, light and love that will
allow us to flee far from our demons, far from our tombs.

❧ 28 ❧

Y ou need patience to do God's will
and receive what he has promised.

HEBREWS 10:36

Patience is a virtue. And of all the virtues out there, perhaps it is the most difficult for many of us to master. We live in a world where many things are instant and having to wait for something, not being able to do anything about it, can be unnerving. We want what we want now.

And so it is that we can be impatient even with the way we grieve. Why does this continue to affect me so? Why can't I feel better about this sooner? Faith is the only antidote to poisonous impatience—faith that God will deliver what has been promised. And faith that God will take care of things on God's time, not necessarily ours.

*Faith is the only antidote to poisonous impatience…
faith that God will take care of things on God's time,
not necessarily ours.*

❦ 29 ❦

O Lord, you have searched me and known me,
you know when I sit down and when I rise up,
you discern my thoughts from far away.

PSALM 139

When as a freshman in college I went away from home for the first extended time, I talked to my father a great deal on the phone. The sound of Dad's voice on the phone could cheer me up, assure me that financial help was on the way, give me sympathy when I needed it, and—perhaps more frequently with a college freshman—give me a kick in the pants when I needed that too. My father had the ability to be able to tell how I felt and what I needed by simply listening to my voice, and even if there were things that I felt I wanted to hide from him, he ultimately ferreted them out of me.

So it is with God. The presence of our God can cheer us up, assure us that help is on the way, give us sympathy, and give us a kick in the pants when we need it. We need only call on Him.

❦ 30 ❦

My soul is like this cloudy, opal ring.

ARTHUR SYMONS

There have been times in my life when I have been awash with sheer joy and my soul seemed to soar in brilliant light, closer to the source of all light. There have been times in my life when I have been weighted down by sorrow and my soul seemed to be buried deep in the darkness. There have been times when I have fallen, not lived up to my potential, and my soul was wounded and needed healing. And when I reflect on it all I realize that the state of my soul has been different from one time to another, but its beauty—a beauty made manifest because of my connection to God—is never in doubt; and like a ring is somehow eternal, and like an opal is captivating even in its cloudiness.

JULY

❧ 1 ❧

With many such parables he spoke the word to them,
as they were able to hear it.

MARK 4:33

Hypostatic union, "Homousias," Tran-signification. People who make
it their business to study theology have all kinds of words to help get
across ideas that are enormous in their implications, as broad as the
very sky. And it's good to study these things, to expand our minds to
the possibilities that exist in our God.

But when faced with all-too-human struggles, ultimately it is not so
much these things that comfort us most, but simple stories of hope and
love Jesus told that—if we let them—can touch our hearts in ways that
nothing else can. Let us never neglect entering into these stories, for they
teach us of God's love in ways we can understand.

❧ 2 ❧

My God, my God, why have you forsaken me?

PSALM 22

The last time I was home I went to the cemetery where my grandparents
are buried. The wind was blowing fiercely over the prairie of central
Illinois, and a mournful howling was in the air all around me. I stood
before their grave, and remembered my grandmother's big arms
around me, my grandfather whistling and playing cards, and at that
moment—regardless of the fact that I was just about a mile from scores
of relatives—I felt so terribly alone in the world that tears seemed to
be the only way I could express the emptiness.

To be human is to know, at one time or another, loneliness. And
although it doesn't make the loneliness easier, it is good for us to realize
that every time we feel forsaken we are participating in that moment
when one man suffered alone against a blood-red sky.

✺ 3 ✺

For she said, "If I but touch his clothes I will be made well."

MARK 5:28

I have a couple of books of my mother's lesson plans from her teaching days. I love to get them out and look at them every now and then. Seeing her handwriting, wondering what she talked about when she had written "current events," imagining just what she did with her free period makes her seem a little more real, a little more present than she ordinarily seems.

Many people don't understand the practice of venerating relics, those bones and other things connected to saints. I have often heard it referred to as morbid, strange. And maybe in some instances it is. But maybe in other instances it is our natural way of trying to make sure a connection is not lost. Maybe it is our way of touching something and being made well.

✺ 4 ✺

During all our distress and persecution,
we have been encouraged about you through your faith.

1 THESSALONIANS 3:7

I recently talked with a young woman whose father had been diagnosed with a terminal illness. I told her—quite sincerely—that I would be praying for him and for the whole family. She seemed as if maybe she was tired of hearing this. She wasn't sure what it meant for people to be praying. What good did it do?

I had no answer for her. I could only tell her that even if I didn't understand how it all worked on God's end, there could be a real strength and comfort in knowing that people were remembering us. Knowing that as we struggle and try to make sense out of it all others are in some way sharing our struggle can make a difference. Even if it doesn't seem that God is helping much through our prayers, we need to know that we are helping one another. And of course when we help one another God is, in the end, helping us after all.

❧ 5 ❧

Gigantic, willful, young,
Chicago sitteth at the northwest gates.

WILLIAM VAUGHN MOODY

One evening years ago my friend Steve and I went to a wonderful play at the Schubert Theatre in my favorite city, Chicago. Afterwards we walked in the delightful weather of a perfect spring night to a nearby restaurant where we spent hours talking religion and literature. At the end even our waitress joined in on the lively discussion. We then walked to Lake Michigan where the waves crashed against the giant rocks, soaking us. We squealed with laughter. It was a perfect night in a fantastic city with a wonderful friend.

I don't get to Chicago too often these days, and regrettably I don't see Steve as much as I would like. But every now and then in the midst of daily traumas, I'll close my eyes and savor this memory. And Steve is somehow here, as is Chicago and its arrogant, willful lake.

❧ 6 ❧

As he walked by the Sea of Galilee, he saw two brothers,
Simon, who is called Peter, and Andrew his brother,
casting a net into the lake for they were fishermen.

MATTHEW 4:18

There is an extreme comfort knowing the Lord chose such ordinary people to be His Apostles. Because if He could take someone as wishy-washy as Peter, or as shifty as Matthew, or as impetuous as James and John and raise them to a new level, then we can hope that He can take us—ordinary people that we are—and raise us to new levels as well. We can have faith that even if we are currently sinking in the depths of an ocean of despair, the Lord's net is quite capable of snaring us and bringing us up to the light of the sun.

7

Making a whip of cords he drove all of them
out of the temple area, both the sheep and the cattle.
He also poured out the coins of the money-changers
and overturned their tables.

JOHN 2:15

The anger that is a result of missed opportunities, wounded pride or
hurt feelings can be intense, but more often than not, it can subside
quickly. Not so with the anger that comes from disappointment—in
others, in ourselves, in the circumstances of life. I think it is just such
an anger that Jesus exhibited in the temple, and it is often the same
anger that accompanies the loss of a loved one. We are disappointed,
and this disappointment gives way to questioning which can give way
to anger. Like Jesus, it seems to me that a worthwhile endeavor is to
find a way that we can express this anger even if it is directed at Him.

8

You have caused friend and neighbor to shun me;
my companions are in darkness.

PSALM 88

"All my friends are dead," a 93-year-old woman once told me. Although
I was only 27 at the time, her words touched something in me. I think
there are times when an innate loneliness can strike us, make us aware
that although we may be surrounded by a plethora of friends and
loved ones, there are still times when we are asked to make part of our
journey alone, in the dark, far from the enlightening presence of those
whom we hold dear.

Many saints throughout the ages could tell us, however, that the
darkness is not an absence, but is filled with a presence beyond all our
imagining. In this sense we begin to see just what a companion darkness
can be.

❧ 9 ❧

To make a prairie it takes a clover and one bee,
One clover, and a bee,
And revery.

EMILY DICKINSON

How to begin again. How to take what was unimaginable, imagine it, realize it, and somehow move forward. How to so change our hearts that the sadness we feel like a thorn can be rendered less sharp and give way to the rose of healing, fragrant with love. How to begin again?

We begin again by small steps. We move forward delicately like a bee hovering near a fragile flower. We change our hearts by allowing glimpses of happiness to bloom there. We begin again by praying that the love which never dies will never die in us, will always sustain us with its delightful fragrance.

❧ 10 ❧

The earth shook and the rocks were split.
The tombs also were opened.

MATTHEW 26:51-52

Upon entering the Archabbey Church, one can't help but notice the giant Christus, or image of Christ, that soars from behind the organ pipes in the apse. He looks a bit stern, standing there in flowing royal robes, His long, bony fingers pointing to a book that He holds bearing the words: *Ego Sum Vita*—I am the Life. It is a definitive, no-nonsense, powerful Jesus Christ that we see.

It seems there has been a tendency in recent years to emphasize the humanity of Jesus, stress just how like us He really was. And although this is clearly of great spiritual benefit, I can't help but take great comfort in the image depicted in our church. Because though I can take comfort in one who suffered, I also delight in one powerful enough to overcome it.

❧ 11 ❧

When it was evening on the first day of the week,
and the doors of the house where the disciples had met
were locked for fear of the [authorities]...

JOHN 20:19

It seems to me they had good reason to be afraid, these disciples of Jesus. Just imagine the thoughts that had to be running through their minds regarding what they had witnessed: Jesus, supposedly the all-powerful Messiah, stooping down and washing feet? Frightening. Jesus, the one to conquer their foes and establish a reign of peace, Himself conquered and beaten by brutal violence? Frightening. Jesus, the way, the truth and the life, stripped of life? Frightening. And add to all that the people in Jerusalem who were hostile to them, and that upon visiting the tomb the body was not where it should have been, they indeed had good reason to be gathered in fear. Fear, after all, is definitely understandable, definitely human.

❧ 12 ❧

We boil at different degrees.

RALPH WALDO EMERSON

I recently talked to a friend who attended the funeral of another friend that I was unable to attend, and the one thing that kept coming up over and over again was the fact that the deceased man's wife didn't shed a tear. My friend was upset by this; how could she not be moved now her husband was gone? It seemed to him uncaring, a bit cold.

I assured him that there is no standard of grief. The person who weeps violently and throws himself on a grave isn't necessarily grieving any more than the person who quietly stands by; it's just that how one person handles it, expresses it, is different from another.

❦ 13 ❦

Then he said to them, "Do you not yet understand?"

MARK 8:21

It is hard for us to imagine how we would have viewed Jesus had we walked the earth with Him like His disciples did. We may be prone to think that if we witnessed Him feeding four or five thousand with just a few loaves and fishes that we would probably get the picture a little quicker than some of them did. Could they not see what He did for them?

Of course, we need ask the question of ourselves as well: Can we not see what He does for us? When our vision becomes clouded due to loss, it is important for us to remember that everything we have comes from God, through Jesus. We are surrounded by His manifestations. Do we still not understand?

❦ 14 ❦

We be of one blood, ye and I.

RUDYARD KIPLING

Last summer I spent weeks studying Gregorian chant at the Abbey of Solesmes in France. The monks there are known for their chant, and the strict formality of their services. I was a nervous wreck, each day struggling trying to figure out which book to use for which service, which utensil to use at dinner, my mind swimming with Latin and French. Fortunately, next to me in choir and at table was a young monk named Frère Bruno who patiently helped me find my place. In the silence of the monastery I would merely look at him, my eyes singing gratitude, his eyes replying (in Latin chant, of course) somehow that he understood.

I am becoming more and more certain that there are no strangers in the world and the intense connection of all humanity can be a strength for us all.

❧ 15 ❧

When he entered the house, the blind man came to him;
and Jesus said to them, "Do you believe that I am able to do this?"
They said to him, "Yes, Lord."

MATTHEW 9:28

If only this faith business were easier. We are expected to have faith in the working of a God whom it is so difficult to see and hear. We are expected to have faith that eventually the just are rewarded and the sinful repaid, even when we can see all kinds of examples of just the opposite. We are expected to have faith that we will somehow be able to rise above the traumas of our lives even when it seems that we are sinking fast. If only this faith business were easier.

It seems pretty easy for the two blind men. They looked to nowhere and no one but Jesus to get what they so desperately needed. "Are you confident that I can do this?" We are. What could be easier?

❧ 16 ❧

And there is even a happiness / That makes the heart afraid.

THOMAS HOOD

I don't remember when I laughed again after the death of my mother. Memories of tears and anger and confusion come readily, but the memory of that first laugh, where the light somehow broke through the darkness around me is lost, although I know it occurred sooner or later. I remember for so long after her death, walking around, feeling that I could not partake in so many of the pursuits that had been the joy of my childhood: baseball, basketball, swimming, bike riding, tag, hide and seek. To give into these, to truly enjoy life again I felt would be a betrayal of who I was and what I felt, even of her memory. But then the laughter came, although I do not remember when, and with its first infectious sound I realized that it was not a betrayal of anything but a recognition of the healing that so needed to happen in my life.

❧ 17 ❧

Ask, and it will be given to you.

MATTHEW 7:7

The impracticality of owning a horse while living in town never really dawned on me, and because of it I asked for a horse over and over again. We had a big back yard, I figured, and—standard kid line—I would feed it and water it and wash it and "You won't even know it's there." Of course, my father didn't go for the whole horse idea—having the ability to see the bigger picture—and so I never got one.

When Jesus says, "Ask and it will be given to you," it is easy for us to point to all kinds of things we have asked from Him and apparently never received. Of course, we need to trust that Jesus has the ability to see the bigger picture and can help us ask the right questions.

❧ 18 ❧

What good is it, my brothers and sisters,
if you say you have faith but do not have works?

JAMES 2:14

We can say that we desire to be one with Christ but until we tear down the barriers between us our words don't mean a whole lot. We can say that whatever we do to one of the lowly ones we do to Him, but if we don't help the lowly ones our words don't mean a whole lot. We can say that whosoever believes in Him shall not die but have eternal life, but if we allow death to have the final say over us our words don't mean a whole lot.

Mourning and questioning go hand in hand, and lamenting our loss with words of confusion and pain does not go against our faith but can be a manifestation of grappling with that faith. But if for one moment we think that death has won, we're clearly not practicing our faith.

❧19❧

He asked them, "But who do you say that I am?"

MARK 8:29

You are at times my greatest frustration and other times my greatest joy. You are one who at times seems to want me to suffer and at other times want to free me from suffering. You are one who at times seems to be more serious than I ever hope to be and at other times seems to be a regular Henny Youngman. You are the one who at times brings me such life, but at other times makes me wonder if you'll be the death of me. And maybe that's the ultimate joke, the ultimate zinger: If I let you be the death of me, you most certainly will be my life. Take my life. Please.

❧20❧

In the morning, while it was still very dark,
he got up and went out to a deserted place, and there he prayed.

MARK 1:35

Life seems to move much more quickly than it used to, and we are becoming masters at cutting back where we need to so that we can fit more in. The world spins at a much faster pace, they say, and you need to keep up or you'll get left behind. "A stitch in time saves nine." The list of speedy aphorisms goes on and on.

I would like to add a different one: If you cut too many corners the piece disappears. In running from event to event, we can run away from that which we really need to face. It's a risk, therefore, to slow down, to face it all, and to listen for God's voice telling us what to do. The answer might be too slow in coming for our tastes, and we might not like what we hear, but ultimately if we can try to absorb ourselves in prayer like the Lord did then maybe we can begin to see meaning in our life as He did in His.

❧ 21 ❧

Summer afternoon—summer afternoon;
to me those have always been the two most beautiful words
in the English language.

HENRY JAMES

It was a time when the hardest decision was whether to swim or to play ball. It was a time when shoes were not needed to go the places I wanted to go. It was a time that, even if it rained, the weather was just perfect for whatever it was I wanted to do. It was a time when I didn't have to do anything if I didn't want to. It was a time—the typical summer afternoon of my youth—when life seemed simpler, more beautiful, and much more hope-filled than it does now.

But memory has the ability to make us long for better times, often not giving thought to the other events of some summer afternoons: the tears, the loneliness. Looking at the whole picture, we begin to realize that the wonder of summer afternoons, the excitement of a world that holds so much possibility—all of this is still with us regardless of how many winters have followed.

*The wonder of summer afternoons,
the excitement of a world that holds so much possibility—
all of this is still with us
regardless of how many winters have followed.*

❧ 22 ❧

Then someone came to [Jesus] and said,
"Teacher, what good deed must I do to have eternal life?"
MATTHEW 19:16

He knew what questions to ask. Encountering Jesus the wonderworker, the man could have asked anything, and I have to imagine there were questions posed to Jesus that didn't make it into the Gospel accounts. But this man knew what questions to ask and so he came to Jesus the Answer with important queries of eternity perched on his lips, curled in confusion and doubt, wonder and revelation.

When so much in our lives can be tempered by loss, we must realize that we too need to know what questions to ask and come to Jesus the Answer. We might not always like what we find, and the manner of lesson might be harsh, but we can rest assured that if we truly listen to Him we'll find out all that we need to know: the confusion and doubt, the wonder and revelation.

❧ 23 ❧

Tell me the tales that to me were so dear,
Long, long ago, long, long ago.
THOMAS HAYNES BAYLY

As I grew older and memories of my mother began to fade, I began asking people who knew her well to tell stories about her. Any story that anyone could tell would be welcomed by me, regardless of how seemingly boring or banal it may have appeared. I realized from an early age that memories and stories were linked to life itself, and if life was to continue in some way—especially my mother's life—there was no other way for me to talk about her, think about her, listen about her.

Some people think that there comes a time to move on from grief, to stop bringing up old pain, and to some extent they may be right. But we must never allow ourselves to move on completely, for life and its stories are too important.

❧24❧

So they kept the matter to themselves,
questioning what this rising from the dead could mean.

MARK 9:10

Here were Peter, James and John. They had just witnessed the transfiguration of Jesus, seeing Him decked out in brilliance, cavorting with the likes of Moses and Elijah. But even after such an elaborate display of divinity, they still had a few questions, primary among them being, "What does it mean to rise from the dead?" They didn't have all the answers, and they needed to make sense of the wonderful confusion that swirled throughout their lives.

We're not different. We are told that when we die we are raised to new life with Jesus. It is in no way a reflection of a weak faith to wonder exactly how all of that works; it is indeed quite the contrary.

❧25❧

Even after a bad harvest, there must be sowing.

SENECA

The other evening, in the middle of singing Sunday Vespers, the sung service that finishes our celebration of Sunday with due solemnity, the organ quit, ceasing to put forth its melodious accompaniment with a bang and a whimper. All eyes turned to the helpless organist, who shrugged his shoulders and gave a clear signal to the community that there was absolutely nothing he could do: just keep singing. And sing we did, without missing a beat.

After vespers had ended, I reflected on what a great analogy for life itself the whole experience was. Because there are going to be all kinds of difficulties that could easily stop us in our tracks if we let them. And though it may be tempting to shut down, to just stop, the real grace comes our way when—somehow—we allow the music to continue through us.

❧ 26 ❧

Simon and his companions hunted for him.
When they found him, they said to him,
"Everybody is searching for you!"

MARK 1:36-37

I used to think that Simon's statement was a bit of an exaggeration. There were so many people in Jesus' day who couldn't have cared less what this strange preacher was up to. There had to have been people who were less than interested in hearing about seeds and yeast, about wedding banquets and long-lost children.

The more I experience human nature, however, I think that it is not so much of an exaggeration after all. Because we all feel empty from time to time. We all seek words of comfort and love, of assurance. And when we find ourselves wanting such things, looking for such things, we are looking for Him. Because He's the only one who can fill the emptiness, who can speak the words we need to hear.

❧ 27 ❧

Nothing that was worthy in the past departs; no truth or goodness realized by man ever dies, or can die.

THOMAS CARLYLE

I was about 16 years old when my grandmother said to me, "Your mother will never be dead as long as you are alive." The context was not as soft and emotional as it sounds. She had observed me butting my way into various conversations, stirring up trouble, and then moving on. But even still I loved hearing it. I loved that even nine years after her death someone was able to make a connection between the two of us. I loved the thought that there was something in me that her own mother recognized as something that was in her as well.

We all carry around traits, quirks, looks, habits—you name it—that those who have gone before carried around as well. Recognizing them, celebrating them, makes death seem less final somehow.

❦ 28 ❦

More things are wrought by prayer / Than this world dreams of.

ALFRED, LORD TENNYSON

In this very practical world of ours that measures success by output, I am often called upon to defend the monastic life. "What do you guys do there, just pray all the time?" is a common question, and no matter how much I talk about the work we do here, people can't seem to understand why we would gather in church four times a day, every day. "How can you get anything done, going to church so much?"

I can't measure out for these people what exactly all that prayer has wrought. I can't point to something specific that has been changed in the world because of it, although I have my suspicions about a thing or two. But I can point to myself and others who somehow see the value in prayer: If it can change people like us, I have no doubt that it can change just about anything.

❦ 29 ❦

The nurse of full-grown souls is solitude.

JAMES RUSSELL LOWELL

There can be a tendency when our souls are aching from loss to surround ourselves with people. If we constantly have people around us, we think we just might not notice the emptiness, or the loneliness will not seem so lonely. And while our family and friends can be enormously helpful, they, in the end, cannot completely fill the void. It is only with a combination of human interaction and being alone with God that we begin to heal. The silence of solitude, though sometimes bitter to swallow, is a necessary medicine for all of us.

❧30❧

[Jesus] said to him "Ephphatha!" that is, "Be opened!
And immediately his ears were opened,
his tongue was released and he spoke plainly.

MARK 7:34-35

"Be opened!" This is wonderful advice, not just for the poor man who couldn't hear or speak, but for all of us, whatever our infirmity. Because to be closed is to stop living. To be closed to love, hope, memories or new ways of doing things is to be like a musician content to merely play the same piece over and over again.

Be opened, the Lord says. Be opened to love, even if it can seem fleeting. Be open to hope, even when feeling despair. Be open to memories, even when they can be painful. Be open to new ways of doing things, even if it's hard to let go of the old ways. By being opened we find the tune can change from the boring music of inertia to the glorious symphony of the love of God.

❧31❧

There is in God, some say, a deep but dazzling darkness.

HENRY VAUGHAN

Many of the greatest mystics in the Christian tradition, those who through their prayer have been able to achieve a particularly intense closeness with God, have also experienced a silence, a darkness, an apparent lack of communication that can be nearly crippling. If we are supposed to pattern our life with our relationship to God in mind, then what does that pattern look like when we are having trouble relating, when we wonder if God is there at all?

The answer is to realize that in silence God can speak more eloquently and beautifully than ten thousand angel choirs. In the darkness God's face can be more dazzling than ten thousand stars. We need not worry about silence and darkness if we realize that God can be silent and dark.

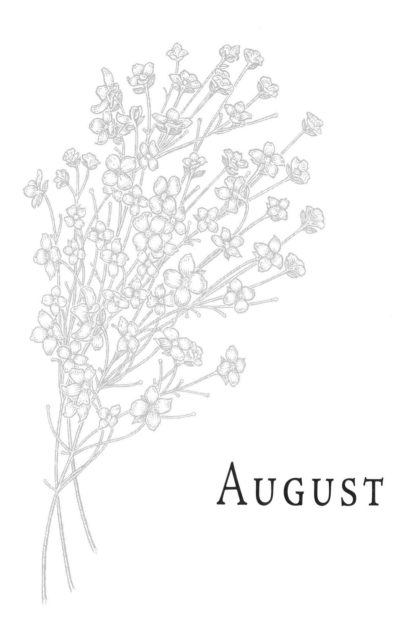

AUGUST

❧ 1 ❧

Every parting gives a foretaste of death
every coming together again a foretaste of the Resurrection.

ARTHUR SCHOPENHAUER

The day before I left for college, I went over to my grandparents' house to say goodbye. My grandmother cried (as I knew she would) and from the sheer amount of tears one would have thought that I was studying overseas rather than a mere hour and a half away. At Thanksgiving break, my Grams smothered me with kisses and tears and sat listening attentively as I regaled her with tales of college life (or sselect tales of college life, anyway).

Four years later it was my turn to cry as her casket was placed in her grave. I knew my tears for her were somehow related to the tears she shed for me when I went away to college. Things sometimes seem balanced in the universe and that our eventual reunion will be just as sweet—both of us smothered in a love that cannot die.

❧ 2 ❧

How great a forest is set ablaze by a small fire!

JAMES 3:6

It's that first step. It's laughing at a shared joke even when nothing but tears have preceded it. It's leaving the house to go out even when you don't want to see another person. It's facing the routine of bills, shopping, errands, even when all of those things seem alien and overwhelming. Whatever the circumstance, it is that first step wherein a world shattered by loss is, for a moment, allowed to coexist with the ordinary world you remember. And in being able to take this first step, no matter how seemingly insignificant, we begin to see that life goes on even if we can't fathom how. With this first step, that which is cold in us begins to feel a taste of the warmth of God's healing fire.

❦ 3 ❦

God is and all is well.

JOHN GREENLEAF WHITTIER

Once I was driving Archabbot Lambert to a meeting that was of some importance for him. It dawned on me—forty miles out and in the midst of horrendous traffic—that there was absolutely no way that we could arrive on time; indeed we would probably be nearly an hour late. My mind kept imagining an enormous board room, with hordes of business-suited people sitting around a table, tapping pencils on the table and looking at their watches. I was a nervous wreck, and it wasn't even my meeting.

In the midst of what I clearly saw to be a trauma, the Archabbot announced to me that he was going to take a nap for a few minutes. And he did, amazingly enough. And it dawned on me how much easier life would be if I didn't spend so much energy fretting about the things I cannot change.

❦ 4 ❦

Draw near to God, and he will draw near to you.

JAMES 4:8

We lament the passage of time, remembering moments in our lives when we were happier. Current struggles only seem to make that happiness seem more distant. We lament the distance that exists between friends and loved ones, as life's roads have taken people in different directions. We lament the distance between who we are and who we long to be, realizing with regret just how often we fall short of the mark. And in all of these distances there is an emptiness, a longing to have something filled.

We sometimes think that there is an enormous distance between God and us. When we sense this distance we need to realize that our God is often expressed in a paradox: Through silence we hear God's voice, through darkness we experience God's light, through emptiness we are filled with His presence.

❧ 5 ❧

You faithless generation,
how much longer must I be among you?

MARK 9:19

The disciples were a good-intentioned lot, but even the best of people can bring about exasperation, as is clearly evidenced in the Lord's outburst. The disciples' inability to see the whole picture was a constant issue that Jesus had to face over and over again, and even though wondering how long He would have to stick with them is perhaps not the epitome of patience, He was always able to stick with them.

There are good-intentioned people in our lives who, sometimes, just don't manage to see the big picture. There are people who want what is best for us but manage to say and do the wrong things over and over again. Our impatience with them can be understandable, but we need to make it our prayer that we can always be able to stick with them.

❧ 6 ❧

Many strokes overthrow the tallest oaks.

JOHN LYLY

When I was growing up, my father was a stickler for making sure we had our napkins on our laps at every meal. It's not that we were a particularly formal family but for some reason the napkin-on-the-lap thing was non-negotiable, as if my father was at least trying to get us to think in terms of manners and other things of bigger importance.

Sometimes the small gestures we make possess a relevance and importance that we only come to realize later. So we must be confident that any step we can make in the direction we need to go is the right step to make, and eventually we'll get to where we're going. I remember this every time I pull out of a fast-food drive-through, making sure my napkin is on my lap before I get on the road.

❧ 7 ❧

Next to theology, I give music the highest place and honor.

MARTIN LUTHER

Every year on Palm Sunday, our schola (choir) sings a three-part, a capella version of the Passion of Jesus Christ, written by our Father Columba. It is wondrous, and the complexity of emotions surrounding the tragic story is not only played out in the text but in the style and tone of the music as well. The notes that surround us paint such a vivid picture of that day so long ago that it is as if we're there, each crescendo a swell in the anger of the crowd, each simple softness an echo of the voice of a dying man.

There are times when I can't put into words how I am feeling, the entanglement of emotions is so rich. At those times I turn to music, realizing that even if I can't find a voice for something, someone else may already have.

❧ 8 ❧

For God so loved the world that he gave his only Son,
that everyone who believes in him may not perish but have eternal life.

JOHN 3:16

He was ubiquitous at sporting events, a ballpark Kilroy, always there: Sporting a rainbow wig, running around to be in front of the camera, holding a large sign that simply read, "John 3:16." How ridiculous he seemed to me, I who like my religious displays in church, preferably with organ music and incense. Indeed, my friends and I used to mock him and imagine alternative signs that we would carry around if we got the chance. We were, quite simply, embarrassed for him.

Maybe that's what he wanted. Because his sign, if nothing else, points to the embarrassing excess of a God for whom death can be an instrument of love. How divinely ridiculous.

❦ 9 ❦

With many parables he spoke the word to them
as they were able to hear it.

MARK 4:33

My friend Phil and I both graduated from small, Midwestern high schools in 1984, so our conversations are filled with allusions to the movies, videos, music and trends that marked those years of big hair and parachute pants. Although we now lead very different lives (he's married with children and I'm a monk) we nevertheless often seem to find common ground because we share the same vocabulary.

Jesus often told stories to His listeners in language that was clearly going to make sense to them, so earnest was His desire to help them know of the wondrous, confusing love of God. That He used stories of vineyards and seeds where we may rely on references to *Brady Bunch* episodes isn't as important as the fact that we continue to teach one another the message in ways that we all understand.

❦ 10 ❦

O that I had wings like a dove! I would fly away and be at rest.

PSALM 55

How attractive a thought, when mired down by the very real sorrows and struggles of life, to imagine soaring above it all. How calming to envision a whole new perspective from up there, where the problems below don't affect us, where everything seems small, where nothing can touch us. And though the tendency to want to get away from it all is natural, and escape can even be good, even doves must eventually land back on the earth, their peaceful cooing expressed in the midst of the harsher sounds of life's struggles.

The wonder is, I think, not that they can fly above it all, but rather that they continue to make such sweet sounds in the midst of it all.

❧ 11 ❧

Scenery is fine, but human nature is finer.

JOHN KEATS

I was looking at photographs that I took one summer while visiting a chateau in the Loire Valley of France. On top of the chateau there is a beautiful view, as the verdant beauty of the valley spills before the eye like an immoderate painting, shapes and colors everywhere. I took out my camera to record the moment. Upon looking at the developed film, I was more than a little annoyed and embarrassed to see that in what would have been the best shot, there is a couple in the corner passionately locked in a kiss that appears to be a bit excessive.

The more I viewed the photograph, however, I began to see that the beauty of the valley paled in comparison to the sheer loveliness of that kiss, because land and buildings can change or be destroyed but love cannot.

❧ 12 ❧

Her sins, which were many, have been forgiven;
hence she has shown much love.

LUKE 7:47

Most of us live with regret: missed opportunities, "what-if's", sorrow surrounding pain we may have caused another. And perhaps the most terrible regret that we face is that regret which surrounds someone who is no longer with us. "If only I could say I'm sorry," we think, "things would be much better."

But we should know the love that spurs us on to want to make things right: This love has the ability to reach back through time and heal what was hurting, restore what was broken. So the key to staring down regret is to make sure that we never stray from love's gentle hope, love's amazing promise.

❧13❧

To me every hour of the light and dark is a miracle,
Every cubic inch of space a miracle.

WALT WHITMAN

Apparently miracles just don't seem to happen as much as they used to. When Jesus was around they were nearly an everyday occurrence. And after His Ascension, the members of the fledgling early Church were known to bring about a few miracles as well. And what about the saints? They are a virtual storehouse of miraculous activity.

But those were simpler times and people were simpler, we say. What many people thought of as miraculous back then can be achieved by other, not-so-spectacular ways today, we say.

That doesn't mean that they're not miracles, if you ask me. Sometimes in trying to explain everything away, we miss sight of just how wondrous the world can be. And just how possible it is for us to receive a miracle when we most need one.

❧14❧

After all there is but one race—humanity.

GEORGE MOORE

I did a summer chaplaincy at Northwestern Memorial Hospital in Chicago a few years ago. Every morning when I would walk to the hospital, I would be besieged by a particular street person asking me for money. I never really knew what to do. Is money what he really needed? Although some of my feelings conflicted, one did not: The man made me painfully aware of the gulf that separated people like him from people like me. His life was so alien to me that I could never even imagine what it was like to be him. We were so different.

Or so I thought. One day I found out that his name was Mark, which was my name at the time, and it dawned on me that this great chasm that I had imagined separating us was not so great at all—he could easily have been me, and I him.

❧ 15 ❧

E'en though it be a cross / that raiseth me;
Still all my song would be, / Nearer, My God, to Thee
Nearer, My God, to Thee, / Nearer to Thee.

SARAH FLOWER ADAMS

I long to be close to You, O Lord, but the trials of life are just too many at times. I long to be close to You, O Lord, but I can't seem to get beyond the pain. I long to be close to You, O Lord, but confusion clouds my judgment, my desire. I long to be close to You, O Lord, but sometimes the suffering is just too much.

If you long to be close to Me, He would say in return, then understand that I am no closer than in the trials, the pain, the confusion, the suffering. If you long to be close to Me, know that, through it all, you already are.

❧ 16 ❧

Sing for joy, O heavens, and exult, O earth,
break forth, O mountains, into singing.

ISAIAH 49:13

I was stopped at a stoplight and turned to look at the car in the lane next to me. Driving the car was a man who was not only singing at the top of his lungs but playing an imaginary set of drums as well. I began laughing, wondering if he knew how ridiculous he looked. Just then he turned and looked at me. Instead of stopping his imaginary rock concert and looking away embarrassed (what I clearly would have done in his position) he just continued to sing, continued to drum, staring into my amazed eyes until the stoplight turned green and we both moved on.

It seems to me we need to take comfort in the fact that there is so much joy in the world, even if at a particular moment it might not be our joy. If we don't feel like singing, let us be thankful that the song is at least on the lips of others.

❦ 17 ❦

To dry one's eyes and laugh at a fall,
And baffled, get up and begin again.

ROBERT BROWNING

"If at first you don't succeed," it is said, "try, try again." And although the sentiment is a good way to go, I'm not sure the saying really gets to the heart of this failing-and-trying-again business. It doesn't seem to take into consideration the metaphorical scraped knees and elbows (and even longer-lasting wounds) that are part and parcel of failing. It doesn't seem to take into account that some of the ways we fail are in our relations with other people, and the confusion, sadness, joy and ending of these relations.

But still, all in all—we must get up and begin again. To not do so is to die.

❦ 18 ❦

By the rivers of Babylon, there we sat down and there we wept.

PSALM 137

Early Christian writers often talk about the "gift of tears," a notion that is perhaps difficult for many modern thinkers to embrace. We live in a society where tears are seen as weakness, surrounded by people who see some sort of courage and strength in not crying.

But these, our ancestors in the faith, knew tears were a physical way of showing just how deeply we have been touched. Touched by sadness. Touched by joy. Touched by confusion. Touched by doubt. Touched by hope. Touched by gratitude. In those places deep within us where tears are born, we are so touched that merely thinking or talking about it doesn't seem quite enough. And so come the tears, a testimony to the God who can touch us to our very core.

❧ 19 ❧

For God is not unjust;
he will not overlook your work
and the love you showed for his sake
in serving the saints as you still do.

HEBREWS 6:10

When I was in the parish I worked with a delightful nun named Sister Justine. Sister Justine was in her 70's, and her main mission was to care for those she referred to as "the old," although some were no older than her. I learned a great deal about true compassion when I would accompany her on her rounds. She offered a listening ear when needed and wasn't afraid to offer some challenging words when there were called for. And when the lives of her flock were over, she offered to read the Scriptures at the funeral.

I used to wonder how she could work so tirelessly with people and then watch them slip away into death over and over again. Then it dawned on me that her caring for the living and her care for them after their death spoke of a God whose care for us is constant and never-ending.

Her caring for the living
and her care for them after their death
spoke of a God whose care for us
is constant and never-ending.

❦20❦

[This grace] has now been revealed through the appearing
of our Saviour Christ Jesus who abolished death
and brought life and immortality to light through the gospel.

2 TIMOTHY 1:10

How hazy it must have appeared to so many of our ancestors, this notion of the resurrection of the dead. In the course of their daily struggles, living life as they had for generations, the questions of eternity had to hang over their heads like a collective fog. What would happen when they died? Would they pay for their sins and the sins of their fathers? Was their hope that their spirit could live on?

While they knew the haze of uncertainty, we are blessed to know the clear light of the Gospel promise of Jesus Christ. Death has indeed been robbed of its power, and even though it takes a terrible toll on us, the living, we must never doubt the illuminating power of that light.

❦21❦

The poetry of earth is never dead.

JOHN KEATS

Some of my happiest childhood memories revolve around time spent at my grandparents' cabin on Patterson Bay, a little bay off of the Illinois River. The days there were magical: fishing, walking and the general running around of which children are masters. My cousin Christopher and I used to walk out into woods that were completely surrounded, for the most part, by water. If I close my eyes I can still get a sense of it: the smell of the water and insect repellant, the sensation of the wet mud oozing through my toes, the feeling of the muggy heat running down my back in rivulets of sweat. So many things in life can be transitory, and it soothes me to know that the bay and the woods and the heat are still there even though my grandparents no longer are.

❧22❧

Jesus, if this is how you treat your friends,
it's no wonder you have so few.

TERESA OF AVILA

"Take up your cross and follow me, mine is the way to life." So goes one of the refrains we sing periodically in church. We have sung it over and over again, and I'm sure most of us don't give too much thought to the words even as we sing them. We can sing of the Cross. We can preach eloquently about how it is the necessary instrument of our salvation. We can agree that without the ugliness of the Cross there could have been no beautiful Resurrection morn.

But in the depths of our hearts it's still pretty hard to take, this Cross business. Couldn't there be a better way to draw closer to Jesus than this?

Perhaps we think there could be a better way. But God obviously does not. In setting the Cross in our midst, He shows us the true meaning of a friendship that never dies.

❧23❧

Who rises from prayer a better man, his prayer is answered.

GEORGE MEREDITH

"Help me heal," I cried to God, and yet my heart still felt broken, my prayer apparently unanswered. "Help me understand it all," I cried to God, and yet I was still filled with confusion, my prayer apparently unanswered. "Help me to accept it all," I cried to God, and yet I still seethed in anger, my prayer apparently unanswered.

And through it all I noticed something happening: I began to heal a bit but not all; I began to understand a bit but not all; I began to accept a bit but not all. My prayers were apparently answered but not all. Not yet.

❧ 24 ❧

[He] consoles us in all our afflictions
so that we may be able to console those who are in any affliction
with the consolation with which we ourselves are consoled by God.

2 CORINTHIANS 1:4

It never seems to get any easier, knowing what to say to people who
have suffered loss in their lives. All too often we stand in a receiving
line at a funeral home and are never entirely certain what we will say
when we get to the grieving family. And when we speak, our words
seem sterile, meaningless, and seem to offer scant solace.

But even if we feel our words leave something to be desired, our
presence does not. Our presence is a reflection of the presence of a God
who will not leave His children alone but desires to be with them in
their grief.

It's all connected: God's care for us and our care for one another. Let
us never forget this, because our care—not necessarily the words that
we say—is what really matters.

❧ 25 ❧

How lovely is your dwelling place, O Lord of hosts!

PSALM 84

I have been in grand, ancient cathedrals, their spires rising to a Heaven
that can seem quite remote, but inspiring nonetheless. I have been in
small country chapels, their cramped spaces suggesting a God who
is very close to us. And in all of them—from soaring gothic heights
to understated simplicity, from gold gilt to time-worn wood—there
is something calming, powerful, promising. That God is present in a
sunset, or a lake, or the laugh of a child is true; but God's presence in
houses of prayer all over the world is unique. Let us never lose sight of
the fact that God's dwelling place is lovely and offers us a solace and
hope that we find nowhere else.

❧ 26 ❧

[Jesus] called his disciples and said:
"I have compassion for the crowd."

MARK 8:1-2

Maybe they were hungry, their empty stomachs growling. Maybe they were searching, their empty souls longing to be filled. Maybe they were sorrowing, their empty hearts longing to beat with love once again. Whatever their needs, He sensed them and He felt pity. He filled that which needed to be filled.

We too face emptiness. And the same pity that Jesus extended to those people so long ago is extended to us as well. If we let Him fill our needs, we too will find that we will walk away from the encounter much the better for it. Our challenge, of course, is that we have to come to Him in the first place.

❧ 27 ❧

For all of us make many mistakes.

JAMES 3:2

I remember my mother told me once to do something insignificant—take off my shoes before coming into the house or pick up some toys—and I ignored her. After she died I began to feel a disproportionate amount of guilt over this one incident. Why couldn't I have done what she asked? I wondered myself. If only I could turn back the clock.

Most of us have a hard time forgiving our own mistakes, but our mistakes can take on epic proportions when they involve someone who is no longer physically around. But we do all fall short in many respects and the things that plague us in regards to loved ones who have gone before us aren't necessarily as terrible as we think. We constantly need to steel ourselves in the practice of putting things into perspective.

❧ 28 ❧

I wept and I believed.

FRANÇOIS RENÉ DE CHATEAUBRIAND

Chateaubriand used these words to describe his conversion to Christianity, and they touch upon a rather ancient tradition: the connection between faith and tears. We live in a world where tears can be misunderstood or considered bad form. But if we profess our faith with our whole heart and soul and body, then the body's expression of grand truths and realities just might take the form of tears. Tears of joy at the wonders of being a child of the light. Tears of gratitude at being uniquely God's own. Tears of sadness at letting go of someone we love. Tears of anguish over pain suffered. And so we can say that we wept because we believed.

❧ 29 ❧

Most people want security in this world, not liberty.

H.L. MENCKEN

Throughout much of grade school and through high school, my father and stepmother left for work before I got out of bed in the morning. As they were preparing to leave for the day, they would yell upstairs to make sure that I was awake. I didn't feel as alone, however, as this may make it sound, because every morning when I came downstairs there was always lunch money and a note waiting for me. The note could say anything from, "Have a good day!" to "Don't forget to unload the dishwasher," but whatever its content it always had the same effect on me, making me feel protected and loved.

Even when God seems far away, the world is filled with signs that we are protected and loved. We must make sure we don't run out the door without paying attention to them.

❦30❦

Sing away sorrow, cast away care.

MIGUEL DE CERVANTES

Brother Matthew admittedly doesn't have the best singing voice in the world. But when Brother Matthew opens his mouth to sing, you can see all over his face that he really believes what he's singing. In the midst of drudgery and routine and work and perhaps even a little sorrow now and then, he nevertheless has the faith to open his mouth and sing, "For His love endures forever!" and I know it's true. Even if I have a hard time seeing (or hearing) that love in my own song, it is a comfort and strength for me to see it and hear it in his. And what a wonderful melody! It is ultimately an echo of the song God sings to woo the world.

❦31❦

The strongest and sweetest songs yet remain to be sung.

WALT WHITMAN

I remember the day my mother died, climbing my favorite tree, the one in between our yard and the yard of our neighbor, Miss Crain. As I perched myself in the midst of the tree's leafy familiarity, I felt as if life would never again be good. How could I ever enjoy a game again? How could I ever really know what it means to love since the one I loved most was gone? It was a sad day: a seven year old had decided that his life was over.

It wasn't over of course. And I don't know if it would have made a difference that day if I could have seen into the future and known of all the games, smiles and love that would come my way. It probably wouldn't have made a difference then, but it does now.

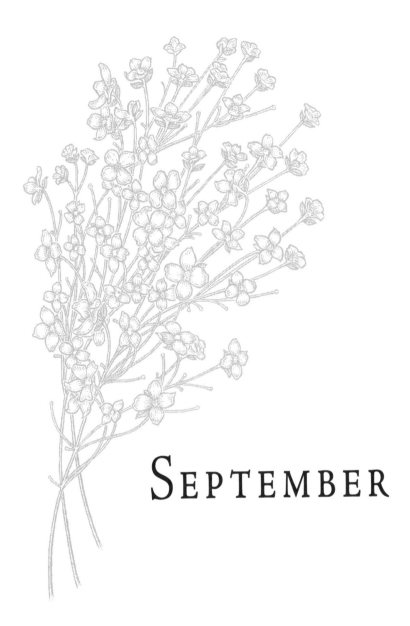

SEPTEMBER

❦ 1 ❦

God is faithful.

2 CORINTHIANS 1:18

God said, "Let there be light," and there was light. God said, "It is not good to be alone, I will make you a partner," and a partner was created. God said, "I will bring the Israelites to a land flowing with milk and honey," and the Israelites settled in just such a place. God said, "I will send them my Son," and Jesus came into the world. Jesus said, "Your sins are forgiven," and they were, they are. Jesus said, "I am the way," and it's true.

If God, through Jesus, kept all of these promises (and countless others as well) then we can be certain that when He said, "Anyone who believes in me shall never die," He meant it.

❦ 2 ❦

I am the vine, you are the branches.

JOHN 15:5

I had never really been in a vineyard before, but not long after arriving at the monastery I was sent to our vineyard to pick grapes for the harvest. On one hand it was an awful experience: sweltering heat, dripping humidity, angry bees and wasps swarming the outer grapes that had burst open. On the other hand it was fascinating, because I could see close up just how reliant upon the vine the branches were.

Another thing I noticed, however, was that the best grapes were the ones that were buried deep within the mass of branches, with the other branches acting as a shield against the severity of the elements. And it dawned on me that it was not only the vine that helps the branches bear fruit, but the branches themselves. Not a bad lesson for us branches.

❧ 3 ❧

For he will command his angels concerning you,
to guard you in all your ways.

PSALM 91

Angels have become big business. What many once considered a quaint little religious belief has exploded into pop-culture's consciousness. We have movies and television shows about angels. We have posters and T-shirts and wristwatches with angels on them. We have books encouraging people to get in touch with the angel inside of them. To be honest, I'm not sure what any of this has to do with the real angels that attend to God. I'm not sure any of it speaks to the deep theological significance of these created, incorporeal beings and their mission—their message—to us.

But it does speak of our need to know that God is watching out for us. It is a comfort to know that—whatever angels do or do not look like—somehow God's care for us extends in ways that we can't know or understand but that is most certainly real.

❧ 4 ❧

There is a wisdom of the head, and…a wisdom of the heart.

CHARLES DICKENS

A few days after my mother died, I remember an adult telling me the past few days had been very hard and tiring for my father, and I needed to be especially good so that he didn't have to deal with any more than he was already dealing with. Even as a seven year old, this made sense to me, seemed to possess a wisdom and common sense that even I could grasp. They went on to say, however, that I shouldn't be crying as much as I was—I should try extra hard not to. Whereas the wisdom of doing all I could to help my father seemed to make sense to me, this seemed a bit harsh; after all I didn't want to cry. I ran off and ran into my Gramps, who took one look at me and knew exactly what I needed. "Let it out, Spark Plug," he said to me. And I did. And with my tears came a recognition of true wisdom.

❦ 5 ❧

Pain is short, and joy is eternal.

JOHANN CHRISTOPH FRIEDRICH VON SCHILLER

With these words von Schiller ended *The Maid of Orleans*, his play about Joan of Arc. And though the story of this heroic girl is inspiring, it is a bit difficult for us to connect with her way of thinking. She heard voices; she was always courageous; she was a saint. Those of us who toil without voices and courage and sainthood might find it difficult to see just how fleeting pain is, especially when we are in the middle of it. Leave that thinking to the saints—I don't want to suffer any more.

However, the exceptional sanctity of Saint Joan doesn't take away the truth of either the transitory nature of suffering or the eternal nature of joy. Perhaps if we wish to make such a connection we should work harder at being saints ourselves.

❦ 6 ❧

He drove out the man,
and at the east of the garden he placed the cherubim.

GENESIS 3:24

I remember thinking during my senior year in college that life could not possibly be better than it was then. I had very little responsibility; I was surrounded by my friends; my family was doing fine. And it was glorious, this constant happiness, this little piece of paradise that I had staked out.

Then it started happening. My grandmother died. My sister got sick. And all of a sudden paradise was no longer my address but a place I used to live. As time continued I found myself longing for those days: Remember our senior year in college?

I realize now that the paradise I perceived was real, but not lasting. How much easier life has been since I accepted that I will never live in paradise again until the end of my life (and then a much greater Paradise), and instead have settled just east of there for now.

❧ 7 ❧

In looking on the happy autumn fields
And thinking of the days that are no more.

ALFRED, LORD TENNYSON

My favorite time of year for walking is the early autumn when it is easy to get lost in the sights and smells of an Indian-summer day. The cool wind blows the aroma of burning leaves and if I close my eyes the smell seems to have a life of its own; it is no longer just a smell, but sights and sounds, colors and memories. The leaves under my feet are musical instruments and I am transfixed by their song. Everything around me attests to one thing: Summer is truly over. This could be happy (a testimony to the wondrous cycle of life) or sad (a testimony to the inevitability of death). Being able to realize that autumn is both, is grace.

*Everything around me attests to one thing:
Summer is truly over.*

❧ 8 ❧

Jacob was left alone; and a man wrestled with him until daybreak.

GENESIS 32:34

What did Jacob think he was doing, wrestling with God? How foolish to enter into such a struggle, wrought as it was with certain strife. So passionate was Jacob's desire to know God, to receive His blessing, that he didn't seem to care what it might look like, how foolish or futile it might appear. Even if Jacob knew that he couldn't win and would most likely end up limping away from the encounter (which he did), he knew that the fight was worth it, that in the struggle could be found grace.

God's will is not always easy to understand, and it is no disrespect to question what's going on in our lives. Like Jacob, we need to have the passion to stick with the fight, to face the hard answers that come about as we wrestle with what God wants from us. That limping grace can be ours as well.

❧ 9 ❧

But Moses said to God, "Who am I that I should go to Pharaoh and bring the Israelites out of Egypt?"

EXODUS 3:11

His mental checklist had the reasons he should not go into Egypt: I am not well-loved in Egypt; it's too far away; my sheep will suffer; I have no great army to help me; I don't possess the necessary eloquence. And to counteract this list, God had a list of his own: I will be with you. I will be with you. I will be with you. Moses was powerless against such a list.

Like Moses, we all too often wonder how it is we can do the things we're supposed to. Some days, just getting out of bed in the morning can be a nearly overwhelming task. And we might have a long list of reasons why we just can't go on.

And God's list remains: I am with you. I am with you. I am with you. And we are powerless against such a list. And in this powerlessness we find strength.

❧ 10 ❧

There's a good time coming, boys! A good time coming.

CHARLES MACKAY

At my mother's visitation, a woman from my church enveloped me in a large hug, smashing my face against her lilac-scented bosom, saying, "You've got your whole life ahead of you, you're going to have a wonderful life!" I didn't particularly want to hear that at the time; I had been hearing far too much of it as it was. In the midst of a natural sadness, the last thing I wanted to reflect on was the fact that my life was going to be wonderful again.

That day a life filled with joy was quite beyond my grasp, but it was clearly reality. The sadness would pass and life would continue. I know now how true that is, that sadness passes, and perhaps I knew it that day as well—even if I didn't want to hear it.

❧ 11 ❧

We are afflicted in every way, but not crushed; perplexed but not driven to despair.

2 CORINTHIANS 4:8

If only there were a better way. If only we could expect to live a life free from affliction, free from doubt. If only there were some other model of how to live, one that didn't include some of the less attractive elements like suffering and death. What would such a model look like, I wonder?

It certainly wouldn't look like the model of Christ, who is the only model for a Christian. That Christ was afflicted but not crushed, and that Christ doubted but never despaired doesn't make our afflictions and doubts any easier. But it does make their outcome more certain, if we believe.

❧ 12 ❧

God gave a Loaf to every Bird
—But just a Crumb—to me —

EMILY DICKINSON

I used to look at my friend Godfrey's life with an admiration that bordered on envy. He came from a wonderful family, and divorce and death hadn't touched it much. There didn't seem to be a lot of the internal bickering and intrigue among his siblings that constantly seemed to rear its ugly head in my family. He was so fortunate, I thought; he seemed to get the whole bread loaf, fresh and warm from the oven.

I know now that all the things that have happened to me, although not always pleasant, nevertheless helped make me who I am and—hopefully—helped make me better. When I long for the whole loaf, it serves me well to remember the crumbs can be pretty satisfying at times.

❧ 13 ❧

The kingdom of heaven is like a mustard seed
which someone took and sowed in his field.

MATTHEW 13:31

The reality of this parable is evident. Two thousand years ago, a man with a simple message of love asked people to look at their world, their God, a little differently. And from that humble beginning in an isolated part of the world came the Church, which has spread that original message over all the earth.

This amazing growth isn't chance: It's pattern. And this pattern is played out over and over again, every time we make small attempts in our life, confident that somehow God can and will smile on our efforts to birth possibilities in us that we ourselves cannot even fully imagine.

❖ 14 ❖

Why stay we on the earth except to grow?
ROBERT BROWNING

We are born on this earth knowing nothing, completely dependent. We grow into childhood and we begin to see how the things that we are learning (tying our shoes, looking both ways before crossing the street) can apparently pay off, and so we are dependent upon others to learn more still. We grow into adolescence and suddenly we find that we know more than anyone else and much of what we are supposed to learn (algebra, Shakespeare) is an apparent waste of time. We grow into adulthood and we realize that there is much to learn if we want to get ahead in the world. And we grow into our old age, once again dependent on others, mindful of all that we have learned, mindful of all that we don't know, mindful that life itself—good and bad—has been a most wondrous teacher, even when we found the lessons harsh.

❖ 15 ❖

A man with God is always in the majority.
JOHN KNOX

"I've never lived by myself before," a widow once said to me. At home, she had been the oldest of eight children; eventually she mothered nine herself. And now her husband was gone, her children were grown, and she was alone. That her children lived not too far away offered scant solace; she would be rattling around her big, old house.

I didn't quite know what to say to her, and she was clearly expecting me to say something. And so I told her what I know to be true: We are never alone, for God is with us. I personally can't always see or hear Him, and sometimes I wonder if He is really there, but I have to believe that He is here all the time. Or some days would be pretty difficult to get through.

❦ 16 ❦

My brothers and sisters, whenever you face trials of any kind,
consider it nothing but joy.

JAMES 1:2

It seems a little optimistic, counting trials as joy. I can understand how trials mold and shape us; I can see how undergoing trials makes us stronger. I can even see that life's sweetness can seem sweeter when it is interspersed with trials. But joy? That seems a little far-fetched.

But a brief glance at the dictionary links joy with a feeling of well-being. Maybe that is not so far-fetched after all, not if we grasp that even in the midst of trials God is with us, teaching us, sustaining us and—in some mysterious way often beyond my understanding—loving us. Our beings can definitely feel joy over that.

❦ 17 ❦

Man was made for joy and woe,
And when this we rightly know
Through the world we safely go.

WILLIAM BLAKE

Expectations can often get the best of us and are often the source of inordinate amounts of disappointment. As children we expect to get everything we ask for at Christmastime and were frequently disappointed in the midst of wonderful gifts. As adults we expect people should be this way or that and we are disappointed in the midst of some wonderful gifts.

When we expect life to be perfect and painless, we can be extremely disappointed. If we pray for the grace to change our expectations it is surprising what gifts we discover. God does not disappoint.

❦18❦

Jesus was praying in a certain place.

LUKE 11:1

For some it's the quiet coolness of an empty church; for some it's the expansive verdancy of a lush field; for some it's a park in a busy city; for some it's a child's room; for some it's the sober serenity of a cemetery. Wherever it is, most of us have that "certain place"—the place where we can be ourselves, the place where we can question life's events, the place where we can remember people, the place where we can express joys and sorrows. And ultimately in being ourselves, in questioning life, in remembering people, in expressing joys and sorrows, we find that our certain place is made special by the God who is most certainly present for all of it—and all of us.

❦19❦

Like the clay in the potter's hand,
so are you in my hand, O house of Israel.

JEREMIAH 18:6

I wonder if the people of the prophet Jeremiah's day found this image of the potter and the clay at all comforting. If they gave much thought to the process by which the clay takes form, they may have preferred a different approach altogether, say a nice painting.

Clay is knocked around, torn off, put back together, and shaped with no apparent regard for the material itself. Parts are torn off and thrown away; more is added later. And then, after all the pushing and pulling and tearing and shaping it is thrown in the fire! What could possibly be comforting about this?

Nothing except, of course, that at the end you have a piece of such beauty that our old lives look plain in comparison...like unformed clay.

❧ 20 ❧

The Lord is my shepherd, I shall not want.

PSALM 23

What a beautiful, familiar piece of Scripture is the Good Shepherd Psalm. What a comfort it has been to countless individuals who take solace in the image of a compassionate Savior gently laying a straying sheep around his neck, bringing him back to the safety, the warmth, the sheer love of the flock. The gentleness of the shepherd is captivating.

But what about those times in our lives which "gentle" doesn't exactly describe? What about those times when genuine struggle and hardship make us long for the answers that don't seem to be on the lips of a soft shepherd? What about when we don't need to be tenderly caressed so much as sternly challenged? The psalm still speaks to us. It's just that at these times the shepherd isn't carrying us, He's pushing and prodding us with His staff.

❧ 21 ❧

The Lord spoke to Moses, "Take the staff
and assemble the congregation…
command the rock before their eyes to yield their waters."

NUMBERS 20:8

It stood there, this rock: large, unyielding, hard, dead. And it stood as a testament to a community that itself had grown unyielding and hard. As if to say to them, "I can bring forth life from even the hardest of hearts," he struck that rock with a staff and from what appeared dead came life spilling out, joining the rivers of their souls.

When we think that life has hardened our hearts, that no one can penetrate them, we are fooling ourselves. Because the same God who brought forth water from a rock and brought forth life from a man's execution can tap into even the hardest of hearts, bringing forth amazing possibilities for us to drink.

❧22❧

The supreme happiness of life is the conviction that we are loved.

VICTOR HUGO

I remember my mother reading to me, with me, sharing the wonders of writing with me for the first time. I remember my grandma baking for me, my tongue enraptured with the sweetness of cinnamon and spice. I remember my grandpa telling me stories, giving me a notion of what it meant to be a part of his family, a part of him.

But those are memories. I also have the recent experience of my father teasing me, making me laugh at my own follies. I have the recent experience of my stepmother bringing cookies and underwear to the monastery, taking care of me. The one thing that ties all of this together is love. And I know that the love of my current experience is the same as the love of my memories, and that it goes on. And this makes me aware of God's love which is clearly stronger than death.

❧23❧

I wish you would bear with me in a little foolishness.
Do bear with me!

2 CORINTHIANS 11:1

Patience is a virtue, but there are times when we are going to be moody, temperamental, overly emotional, disagreeable and just downright hard to be around. And all these things can be multiplied ten-fold when they come on the heels of (or particularly because of) loss in our lives. But just as we are patient with the shortcomings of those we love, we need to understand that they will be patient with us. And if there are times when we are not the best people we could be, so be it. We'll get better with a little patience.

❧ 24 ❧

The whole of history is incomprehensible without [Jesus].

ERNEST RENAN

When I was in grade school, we counted ancient years in terms of "B.C."—Before Christ. This accounting seemed to be fine with me and most everyone I knew, but by the time I got to college, "B.C." had become "B.C.E."—Before the Common Era, and something seemed to be missing. It seemed to me that by adding the "E" we were taking away the context of most of the western history of the last 2000 years.

If we believe that history is incomprehensible without Him, how much more are our very lives incomprehensible without Him? We cannot make sense of the things that happen to us in this world without Him, who is the very context of the world, and time, and history.

❧ 25 ❧

Soldiers of Christ, arise,
And put your armor on.

CHARLES WESLEY

In days gone by there seemed to be a lot more battle imagery when dealing with matters of faith. The early monastics went into the desert to battle demons. Those confirmed during a particular time in history were encouraged to become Soldiers of Christ, fighting the battle of faith. In recent years, however, much of this battle talk has gone out of fashion, probably due to the paradox of the Prince of Peace encouraging a fight.

But a fight it can be, this battle with forces in the world that would promote darkness over light, despair over hope. And so maybe it is not such a bad thing to ready ourselves for the battle, armed not with weapons of destruction but with righteousness, faith and hope—armaments worthy of our King.

❦26❦

Although the world is full of suffering,
it is full also of the overcoming of it.

HELEN KELLER

Her world was not, as it is for so many young people, a bright portrait of stunning possibilities; it was a cruel montage of black on black. She heard not the enticing music of reckless joy but only the mocking of silence. She spoke not in the trilling arrogance of freedom but in the labored breath of bondage. But in spite of it all, Helen Keller was able to rise above her suffering and offer hope to many people.

The courage and strength of conviction that enabled her to achieve so much also rests in each of us. To tap into it we need only use our eyes to see what is of ultimate importance, our ears to hear the true message, our lips to speak of the confusing brilliance of a love that never dies.

❦27❦

I live and love in God's peculiar light.

MICHELANGELO

The lines are memorized. The costume adjusted. And then with a rush of adrenaline, the actor steps onto the stage. In the harshness of the lights, he makes us believe he is someone he is not: Hamlet, Othello, Stanley Kowalski. And as long as they are all there, these masks that conceal who he really is, we believe he is actually someone else. Not even the light can expose his secret.

God's light is different. Because unlike the light of the stage, God's light—God's love—penetrates our deepest selves. Our masks do nothing to conceal who we are from Him or who He is from us. In the authenticity that light calls forth we bring everything we are—joys, sorrows, energy, sloth, faith, doubt—and hold it up to be illumined.

❧28❧

The night is dark, and I am far from home; Lead thou me on!
JOHN HENRY CARDINAL NEWMAN

Just a few hours after my mother died my father took my brother and me for a milkshake at Deck's Drug Store, as he had done so many times. As I walked into Deck's I felt as if I had never been there before. The familiarity of this treasured place had disappeared. News of the death had reached the drugstore before we had, and my dad, brother and I were met by the red, puffy eyes of other patrons who had been crying. Why were they crying? I wondered. It was my mother not theirs. Dad told us that we had to be brave; I wasn't allowed to cry.

But later, back home, I ran to my climbing tree and there, above it all, I was able to cry out in sheer anger at a world that would leave small boys motherless. And I could do this because I was home, where I could be myself.

❧29❧

I love everything that's old:
old friends, old times, old manners, old books, old wines.

OLIVER GOLDSMITH

There are those who would say that dwelling on the past is a waste of our time, that the things and people who have gone before us will never again return and so we should forget them. I would agree that dwelling in the past—that making those people and events from the past our measuring stick for absolutely everything in the present—is not the healthiest of attitudes.

But there can be no denying that within the old times lie important keys to our current times and to our future. If we are to understand ourselves, we clearly need to understand where we've been. If we are to understand the influence others have had on us, we clearly need to understand where that influence began. If we are to understand how to live without some of the people and things we once held so dear, we need to understand what it meant to live with them.

☙30☙

I want me, 'twas the Lord. I always told him, "I trust to you.
I don't know where to go or what to do,
but I expect you to lead me," and he always did.

HARRIET TUBMAN

After my ordination I had planned out the next 50 years of my life with precision. I knew exactly where I wanted to be, what I wanted to be doing, and exactly how to get there. God had a place in it all of course but I discerned His will for me to be just a reflection of what I wanted for myself.

Two years after I was ordained I was diagnosed with cancer, and all my plans were cast into confusion. Maybe things were not as settled as I had naively imagined. Maybe God's will was really God's and not my own. I had no choice but to follow His lead, as painful as it was.

All kinds of things can happen that turn our lives upside down. The only sure way to right them again is to trust God to lead us out of it all. He always will.

OCTOBER

❧ 1 ❧

Love kindled by virtue always kindles another,
provided that its flame appear outwardly.

DANTE ALIGHIERI

Maybe it's the soft touch of a mother, melting away fear with the strength of an embrace. Maybe it's the encouraging words of a father, making the harshness of the world seem not so debilitating. Maybe it's the passionate clasp of a lover, whose arms bring about the certainty of acceptance. Whatever the case, most of us have been blessed at one time or another with manifestations of love. And what a difference they can make in our lives, what comfort and certainty they can provide especially in times of suffering and doubt.

And—the cycle goes—when we have been touched in some way by love, we need to touch others. To do so keeps love alive in an all too hostile world. To not do so is nothing short of ingratitude.

❧ 2 ❧

Do not press me to leave you or to turn back from following you!
Where you go, I will go; where you lodge, I will lodge;
your people shall be my people, and your God my God.

RUTH 1:16

How much easier it would have been for Ruth if she had just gone back home. Widowed, among a strange people with a strange God, with no land to call her own and no prospect of finding a husband through regular channels, it would have been so much easier for her to return to what had once been her home, find a life for herself there, and begin again. But Ruth clung to her mother-in-law uttering powerful words of fidelity, thus clinging to her God and His strange ways.

There are times when it would be easier for us to go back to our old ways, to turn our back on this strange God. But like Ruth, we need to realize that the real freedom, the real growth, comes not in freeing ourselves from Him but in clinging to Him.

❧ 3 ❧

When other helpers fail, and comforts flee,
Help of the helpless, O abide with me.
HENRY FRANCIS LYTE

I first met Alice when she was nearing the day of her death from lung cancer. Thrice married and thrice divorced, with no children, she was crusty, angry and utterly alone. At first she didn't want to talk with me; I represented an organized religion that she wanted no part of. More and more I managed to hear her story though, and I was saddened by how lonely she made life sound. I made a resolution that she would not die alone, that I would be there.

Alice died while I was at a nearby restaurant, having dinner with friends. The next day, hearing of the loss, I was angered and distraught—I didn't want her to be alone—and I told the floor nurse how upset I was that no one had called me.

"She didn't die alone," the nurse told me. "Jesus was with her."

I believed her.

❧ 4 ❧

Save that from yonder ivy-mantled tow'r
The moping owl does to the moon complain.
THOMAS GRAY

In many circles it is an unpardonable offense to complain about anything, with the possible exceptions of the government and the Church. Everyone has their own problems, some would say, so I am not particularly interested in hearing yours.

But disappointment, regret and pain are a part of the human existence. And if we do not express our disappointment, regret and pain to others they can—in the unchecked recesses of our hearts and minds—build up so that they become distorted. Better to risk mildly annoying others with our complaints than allow those complaints to control us.

❦ 5 ❧

A good book is the best of friends, the same today and forever.

MARTIN FARQUHAR TUPPER

Every year, immediately after Easter, I read *The Wind in the Willows*, the children's book by Kenneth Grahame. My annual reading of it marks the passage of time, and I bring with each reading another year of experiences, of good times and bad times, that makes me view the story and its delightful characters in new and different ways. My life may change drastically from year to year, but I know that Mr. Mole and Mr. Rat will remain constant, though I may view them differently over time.

In a world where far too much is transitory, we need to find something that we know will always be there. A book is as good a place as any to start.

❦ 6 ❧

Ad astra per aspera.
[To the stars through hardships.]

LATIN PROVERB

Sir Edmund Hilary's reported answer as to why he climbed Mount Everest ("Because it's there") seems at first glance to lack substance. He spent years in preparation and great amounts of money. He endured great physical struggles—even death. And all of it because it was there? Many things in life are there, it doesn't necessarily mean we are going to tackle all of them though.

But even if the literal logic of the statement is lacking, the metaphorical power of climbing the mountain suffuses it with great symbolism. Because like that mountain—just there—so too are the small and not-so-small challenges we face every day. And we scale them because they are there, because not to would be to allow life to defeat us. Because walking around the mountain is not always an option.

❧ 7 ❧

Choose life so that you and your descendants may live,
by loving the Lord your God, obeying him,
and holding fast to him.

DEUTERONOMY 30:19-20

Life's choices used to be so much simpler: What TV show am I going to watch after school? Will I go for a bike ride or swim today? What shirt am I going to wear?

As I grew older the questions became more demanding: Where am I going to college? What am I going to major in? What am I going to do with my life? What role does God play in any of this?

But in it all—from the simplest questions to the deep, existential pondering of life and vocation—the choices, though not always simple, are nonetheless clear. We can choose to give into God's life, loving and holding fast to Him even when we don't understand Him, or we can choose to have no part of Him, the ramifications of which are death. It is in living out this basic choice that all of life's questions get answered.

❧ 8 ❧

The music in my heart I bore
Long after it was heard no more.

WILLIAM WORDSWORTH

I remember distinctly the night before I began first grade, my mother sang to me before I went to bed. The song was a familiar tune but she had changed the words to fit the solemn occasion of my starting school. I remember her voice as being lovely, soothing, quite melodious. I have often been asked where I got my singing voice from and based on this experience I always replied that I got it from my mother.

My sister recently told me that our mother's voice was not quite as sweet as I remembered it. At first I was devastated, but the more I considered it didn't seem to matter all that much. That her song is in me is undeniable, and this makes it sweet nonetheless.

❧ 9 ❧

If a tree dies, plant another in its place.

CARL VON LINNÉ

It's easy to speak about trees but it's naïve to think that this analogy can be extended to people. Or is it? It is true that when we have to say goodbye to a loved one we take leave of so much: companionship, security, connectedness, support. But what about love, memories, laughter, inspiration? What about recognizing those traits within a person that so affected us, and carrying those traits with us until we join them in death's finality?

In recognizing that which lives on after a person dies—by celebrating it—we are planting the seed of healing in our lives, making sure that love continues and grows anew.

❧ 10 ❧

'Tis always morning somewhere in the world.

RICHARD HENRY HENGIST HORNE

I hated going to bed as a child—still do—especially in the summer months. Summer days were filled with such wonder and action that the setting of the sun signaled a disappointing end. Playing our games, we would keep one eye on the game and one expectantly on the western skyline, praying for the sun to cease its downward trek, dreading that moment when mothers and fathers and older sisters began yelling out our names so that washing up could commence.

It was a comfort to me in those days to look to where the sun was setting and imagine that over there, beyond it, a summer's day was just beginning for some lucky kid. Although the odious tasks of washing up and brushing teeth awaited me, I liked knowing that it was a new day for someone else.

❦ 11 ❦

We are going up to Jerusalem.
MATTHEW 20:18

It was in Jerusalem that it would all happen: the condemnation, the mocking, the flogging, the pain, the death. Jerusalem, that seductive city, had seen the death of many prophets. But instead of shying away from it, instead of bypassing this city and all the terror it would soon hold, Jesus told the Twelve what the ultimate price for following Him was to be: They were going to Jerusalem. It was a heavy price to pay.

It is still a heavy price to pay for all of us who, trying to face the struggles of our own Jerusalem, often feel burdened by the weight of the journey. Our only hope, our only consolation, is the same hope and consolation of the Twelve—the hope and consolation of so many people before us who do not make the journey alone.

❦ 12 ❦

The whole secret of the study of nature
lies in learning how to use one's eyes.
GEORGE SAND

One rite of passage at St. Anthony High School is the sophomore-year bug collection. In the months before the collection is due it is not unusual to see mothers clandestinely trading margarine containers and baggies in the grocery store as if trafficking in some contraband substance. "I'll give you this Japanese beetle. Do you know anyone who has a horse fly?" Once a year students and their parents become experts at seeing minute differences between the different varieties of bugs: a mark here, a wing shape there.

It seems to me that human nature requires just such scrutiny. And so if we find ourselves struggling where others have seemingly glided, we need to realize that perhaps we're just a slightly different variety of bug.

❦ 13 ❦

You are the salt of the earth.

MATTHEW 5:13

"He's the salt of the earth," I've heard many times, and I always smile and nod as if I know exactly what it means. But besides the obvious—that people who are the salt of the earth are good people—I'm a little unclear of what being salty signifies. I suppose that if salt makes bland food better, then those who are the salt of the earth somehow make the world in which we live better. It follows then that if we need to season the sorrow that life all too often puts on our plate then we should probably seek out these people for help.

❦ 14 ❦

To what can I liken you
that I may comfort you, O virgin daughter Zion?
For vast as the sea is your ruin; who can heal you?

LAMENTATIONS 2:13

Their wailing was great: eyes worn out from weeping; people sitting in dust; infants not having enough food; tears flowing like rivers, day and night; death and destruction. And in the midst of this unparalleled suffering a question arose: Who can heal you? Even in the midst of their anguished cries the question was cried out in a way that showed they already knew the answer.

We all have our share of lamentations—great and small alike. In the midst of them, let us never fear to cry out that same question: Who can heal us? And let us pray for the grace to already know the answer.

❧ 15 ❧

The sky is the daily bread of the eyes.

RALPH WALDO EMERSON

Just off the monastery courtyard is a place called the Belvidere, a high-arched area where one can sit and look at the valley below without being exposed to the harsh elements. It is ideal for storm watching; to sit, sipping a cup of coffee and watch the sky change from gray to indigo, with large, fast-moving clouds forming patches on its darkened fabric. And after a storm has passed, what delight there is in seeing the first streaks of color peek through the clouds, the rays of the sun piercing it like shards to shattered light.

It's all there—the good and the bad—in the beauty of the sky. How often do we walk under its majesty and not once look upward to revel in such a gift?

❧ 16 ❧

The stone that the builders rejected
has become the chief cornerstone.

PSALM 118

The U.S. Hockey Team scoring the winning goal against the favored Russians; the small-town basketball team winning the state tournament; the cyclist overcoming cancer to win the Tour de France. The world of sports is filled with such stories, stories of underdogs, of people who conventional wisdom said shouldn't have won but who ended up winning nonetheless.

And who doesn't love such a story? It touches something within us that makes us believe, if only for an instant, that absolutely anything is possible when the human spirit is pushed to excel; that even the unlikeliest of people can achieve what had once been thought to be impossible. It goes to follow, of course (even though we don't always see it), that if others can do it we can as well, even when the task seems impossible.

❧17❧

Life is made up of marble and mud.

NATHANIEL HAWTHORNE

I have pictures in my office of vacations and parties that I have attended over the years, beaming faces stare back at me with sheer, unadulterated joy. Periodically I find myself looking at these pictures, trying to remember what it was to be that carefree, that relaxed, that happy. Wondering why life can't be more like that and less like what it often actually is.

These thoughts come all too frequently when we are down, obscuring that life is filled with good and bad alike and we won't see never ending happiness until we pass from this life into the next. Maybe alongside photographs of smiling happy faces we should include a few pictures of frowns, or people we don't care too much for, just to make sure we keep a balanced view of both the marble and the mud.

❧18❧

It's hardly in a body's pow'r.
To keep, at times, frae being sour.

ROBERT BURNS

I drove over to Ed's house as soon as I heard of his wife's death. A couple of his children had already arrived and were hovering about him, tending to his needs in that lop-sided way that adult children can have with their parents. I went into the living room, walked up to his recliner, and asked him how he was doing. He resolutely refused to take my hand and bellowed at me, "How the hell do you think I'm doing, you idiot?" His children were mortified, and began talking to him like he was an unruly child, "Dad, you shouldn't talk to Father that way."

I acknowledged that it was indeed a stupid question, one which maybe even called for such an outburst. We are all human and prone to anger, and I think maybe it was just a time for Ed to be sour. And for me to hear about it.

❧19❧

"Let anyone among you who is without sin
be the first to throw a stone at her."
And once again he bent down and wrote on the ground.

JOHN 8:7-8

There were strict laws against the act in which the woman had been caught, and those laws were to be harshly enforced: She was to die. But up against this man Jesus, the way things had to be done didn't seem so certain. His ways outshone the darkness of their laws, of their minds. To their definitions that day he added a far more encompassing one: God's eternal mercy. And they walked away scratching their heads as he scratched in the dirt.

In the midst of grief, the pressure to do and say the right thing can be enormous. Grieving people by definition are to act a certain way, do certain things, and not do others. But these definitions mean nothing when compared to the merciful love of a God who would tell us that we, if we are mindful of His presence in our lives, are grieving appropriately.

*In the midst of grief,
the pressure to do and say the right thing can be enormous.*

❦20❦

The long sobs
Of the violins
Of autumn
Pierce my heart
With monotonous languor.

PAUL VERLAINE

My mother's favorite season was the autumn, and not surprisingly many of my memories of her center around a season that is filled with dying and color. But also not surprisingly, it is the time of the year that I seem to miss her most. The cool air, the falling leaves, and the colors of change seem to sing to me of her all-too-short presence in my life, and her all too-long-absence. And every year as the summer packs its cloaks of hot, dark green, and autumn replaces them with her aging vestments, I know I'll feel it all the more acutely, this loss. But I also know that my mother is powerfully present, as I realize the colors are still beautiful even if viewed through eyes blurred by tears.

❦21❦

Come, let us return to the Lord.

HOSEA 6:1

God's love for His people can read like a bad romance novel: He woos them, they turn away; He gets angry at them, they repent; He takes them back, they turn away again. How aggravating it can be for us to read of the constant foibles of our ancestors, they who didn't seem to get the picture of how God wanted to be an intimate part of their lives. Why did these stiff-necked people forsake God over and over and over again? Didn't they have any sense?

On one hand, no. Their sense was lacking. But on the other hand, they at least had the sense to know that even if they blamed Him for their ills, they could turn to Him at any time. How easier life would be for us if we always realized that.

❧ 22 ❧

Life does not cease to be funny when people die
any more than it ceases to be serious when people laugh.

GEORGE BERNARD SHAW

Lucy in the chocolate factory, feverishly shoving chocolates into her mouth; "Did you hear the one about the travelling salesman?"; a pie in the face; crazy Uncle Ron's antics at the family reunion. Life is filled with images and instances that can bring about a dose of that most precious medicine, laughter. To let any of them slip by without giving into them, relishing them, is to be like a child stubbornly refusing to take a spoon of cough syrup, allowing its sweet stickiness to temper that which hurts most in us.

❧ 23 ❧

Glorious things of thee are spoken,
Zion, city of our God.

JOHN NEWTON

I had a disgruntled parishioner once complain to me that I did not preach enough about Heaven. As he put it, people needed to know that all the muck we had to put up with in life was going to count for something in the end, so I needed to talk more about Heaven, the New Jerusalem, our eternal reward.

Not long after this his wife died after a protracted battle with cancer. I went to his house as soon as I received the news, and while consoling him he said, "I know she is in Heaven." I wondered to myself how he knew this if preachers like myself didn't talk enough about Heaven. As if reading my thoughts he said, "All of that goodness that was in her has to go on."

Apparently I didn't need to preach to him about Heaven; he preached to me.

❧ 24 ❧

Every man loves what he is good at.

THOMAS SHADWELL

We pride ourselves on our accomplishments. Most of us strive to be the best we can be at what it is we do, and it is a good feeling to know that we have accomplished something, that we have done our homework and are prepared to move forward into the realm of success.

That is why when we grieve it can be unsettling. No matter how much we prepare, no matter how well we say we can take care of things, loss is such an all-encompassing notion that we can never really be prepared, never really know whether our accomplishments in this area are going to bear the fruit that we hope for.

There is no guarantee that we will be good at grief, and we don't like that. But if we move forward with the Lord, we can be assured that He will see to it that we will do the best we can.

❧ 25 ❧

Lead, kindly Light, amid the encircling gloom;
Lead thou me on!

JOHN HENRY CARDINAL NEWMAN

A couple of years ago the power went out in the monastery, affecting even the emergency exit lights. I fumbled my way out of my room to complete darkness—I literally could not see my hand held up in front of my face. How terrifying was that darkness! I turned to go back to the familiarity of my room when I realized that I had walked too far and could not distinguish one door from another. Way off in the distance though I saw a small point of light, perhaps the pen light of a fellow stumbler. Whatever the case, it dawned on me that even in extreme darkness the smallest light could act as a veritable beacon of hope. And so I walked toward it and felt better somehow, even though I didn't know for sure what I would find when I reached it.

❦26❧

But I chose you out of the world.
JOHN 15:19

So often we hear the word "vocation" used in connection with ministry ("He has a vocation to be a priest") or with a career ("She has a vocation to be a teacher"). The concept of vocation goes far beyond this, however. From the Latin "to call," vocation describes the answer in all of us to do what it is we are supposed to do and—to borrow from the Army—be all that we can be. At the root of every Christian call is the One who calls us. The Lord may not call us to do enormous, public things, but He calls all of us to do something. He knows how unique we all are, and He specifically chooses us to do particular things, to bear certain crosses. When we feel it may just be too much for us we need only remember that we were chosen for our lives and obviously we can handle that to which we have been called.

❦27❧

On the sabbath day, we went outside the gate
by the river, where we supposed
there was a place of prayer.
ACTS OF THE APOSTLES 16:13

Some of us prefer to pray in churches, where the quiet of stone and wood help us listen better. Some of us prefer to pray driving down the road, where the hum of the motor and road are a psalm to the continuity of God. Some of us prefer to pray lying in our bed at night, where we can imagine ourselves falling asleep in God's loving arms.

Prayer—that communication between us and God—cannot be limited to a particular time or a particular place. When we begin to understand this we begin to see God everywhere. And if we can see God everywhere we stand a better chance of experiencing His love and comfort when and where we need it most.

❦28❧

Who loves a garden still his Eden keeps,
Perennial pleasures plants, and wholesome harvest reaps.

AMOS BRONSON ALCOTT

I'm not good with gardening but I recognize its merits. Brother Flavian toils in our rock garden and people come from all over to see it, even to have their picture taken in it. Brother James is refurbishing the garden in a courtyard where people often sit under the cloister walk when it rains, watching the water bead on the lush green life. And although I tend to have an ill-effect on plants of any kind, there is something to be said about a garden, and so I am grateful for the presence of the gardeners among us. Besides the beauty that exists in gardens, they are living proof of something we all need to remember from time to time: Life can spring from even the most barren patches if we but care for it. What a merit there is in this indeed.

❦29❧

One crowded hour of glorious life
Is worth an age without a name.

THOMAS OSBERT MORDAUNT

As I write this I have a terrible cold, and have to stop writing every three minutes or so to blow my nose. I am behind schedule on this book you are now reading, and have been working rather late hours for some time to try and get it finished. The skies are turning nearly black with clouds and the wind is picking up, making me think that most certainly an ugly storm is on its way. It is not, in short, a good day.

At the same time, every fifteen minutes I hear the bells chime and no matter how often I hear them, they're still lovely. There is a seminarian walking down the hall outside my office whistling what sounds to me like Beethoven's lovely "Emperor Concerto." And all of it goes into the mix so I realize that—even in the darkest of days—goodness and love are all around.

❧ 30 ❧

Moses said to God,
"Who am I that I should go to Pharaoh,
and bring the Israelites out of Egypt?"

EXODUS 3:11

"Who am I?" he said, eyes and hands stretched to Heaven. The gesture was either praise or a shrug. "I am one person. I have my own problems, my pastures to look over, my own sheep to tend to, my wounds to heal. I am not sure I can do what it is you want me to do. I'm not sure I can go the way you want me to." And to all of his concerns, God gave the answer: "I will be with you." And He was.

"Who am I?" we may ask, our hands stretched to Heaven in either a gesture of praise or one that just might resemble a fist. "I am one person. I have my own problems, I am trying to navigate through these dark pastures of grief. I'm not sure I can go on like you want me to." And to all of our concerns, God gives his answer: "I will be with you. "And He is.

❧ 31 ❧

No longer shall your name be Abram,
but your name shall be Abraham.

GENESIS 17:5

"I will never call you Alaric," a friend told me after I received my new name at the Profession of Monastic Vows. And I understand that changing one's name is difficult for people to understand. The notion of beginning a new phase of a relationship with God (like Abram / Abraham) is not an easy one to grasp, and so many of us monks have to be content, I suppose, with wondering who in our life is going to call us what.

The fact remains, however, that growing closer to God can change us in a fundamental way. And although we needn't necessarily desire to change our name, perhaps it would serve us well to change some of the adjectives we use to describe ourselves as we change from "sinner" to "forgiven;" "grieving" to "understanding;" "lonely" to "lover."

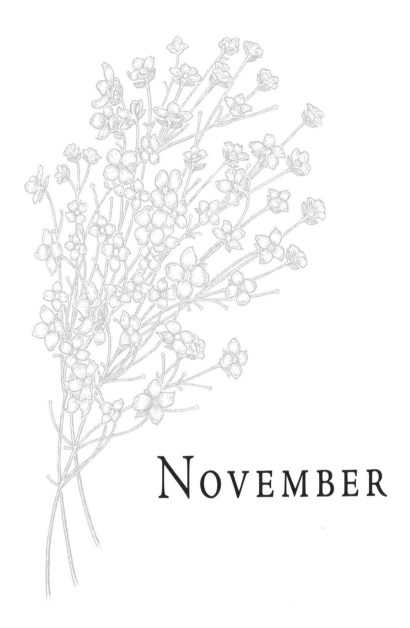

NOVEMBER

❧ 1 ❧

O Lord, I want to be in that number
When the saints go marching in.

AMERICAN SPIRITUAL

We've had fat saints and skinny saints; we've had serious saints and saints with great senses of humor; we've had poor saints and rich saints; we've had saints with ordinary names such as Mark, John, Elizabeth and Mary, and saints with names that are a bit more out of the ordinary like Fidelis of Sigmaringen, Fedlimid, Guthlake, Odo and Odilo.

As different as the saints were, they all had one similarity: They all believed that Jesus was Lord and they tried their best to follow Him in everything they did. They made mistakes and they might have faltered now and then but they all tried to follow Him and keep Him constantly in their hearts and minds. And those who do this, the Lord promises, will be blessed by Him for all eternity.

❧ 2 ❧

A sower went out to sow.
And as he sowed, some seeds fell on the path.

MATTHEW 13:3-4

"You never know," Jesus seems to be telling us in this parable. You never know, given the right climate, the right soil, the right amount of rainfall, if something just might come of it.

And so our smallest actions could bring about great results. Our little gestures moving through grief to acceptance might not seem like a great deal at first, but if we have faith that the Lord can provide the correct climate, soil and rainfall, we can believe that our smallest efforts will yield more than we would have ever imagined.

❦ 3 ❦

I look upon every day to be lost,
in which I do not make a new acquaintance.

SAMUEL JOHNSON

I met Ellen at—of all places—a monastery in France. I went there to study Gregorian chant but much more seemed to happen. I walked away from the experience with a new friend, someone whose views on life I find interesting and who doesn't mind listening to my views.

I met Neal at my monastery. I was meeting him to give him an interview on Gregorian chant, but much more happened. I walked away from the experience with a new friend, someone whose take on life is just different enough from mine to make it interesting and similar enough to make it compatible.

God continually sends people into our lives. If we do not see them as extensions of His care for us, we are missing a great deal of grace.

❦ 4 ❦

What wisdom can you find that is better than kindness?

JEAN JACQUES ROUSSEAU

Her name was Kristy and I knew very little about her. I knew she was the only other second grader who seemed to have an appreciation of the Beatles akin to my own, since she brought Beatles albums for Show and Tell three times. I knew she was of a different religious background than most of the people at my school, since she couldn't say the Pledge of Allegiance and had to leave during Halloween parties. I knew she was what we called one of the "slow" kids since she went to reading class with a different teacher.

And then one day, months after my mother died, she asked me if I missed my mother, something no one else in my class had done. When I told her I did, she offered me a fun-size candy bar, and in this little act of kindness I saw that I knew a great deal more about her than I thought.

❧ 5 ❧

God is love—I dare say.
But what a mischievous devil Love is!

SAMUEL BUTLER

When I was a junior in high school I fell in love for the first time. Her name was Nancy. There was something terribly urgent about the whole affair, and this mysterious love seemed to infect every aspect of my life. In English class it seemed to me that Macbeth was so tragic because he just hadn't really found the right woman. At the dinner table I would stare dreamily into my mashed potatoes, wondering what she was eating at her house, longing for the end of supper when I could call her and ask her myself. Every aspect of life seemed charged with an excess of energy.

When I read that God is love, I think sometimes it bears more resemblance to this urgent kind of love than the more civilized, polite love with which we often equate God.

❧ 6 ❧

Love truth, but pardon error.

VOLTAIRE

One Thanksgiving when my niece Kristen was a little girl she knocked a crystal goblet off the table, causing it to break against the leg of a chair. Her response to her mother's stern stare was, "I only wanted to help!" And of course she meant no harm and was quickly forgiven.

It may be that there are loved ones who have contributed to parts inside of us where we sense brokenness. These faults can seem multiplied and worsened after their death, because there seems to be no way of addressing the hurt caused. There is perhaps nothing that can put all the pieces back together, but praying for the grace to forgive can at least help us remember the beauty that was once part of the crystal.

❧ 7 ❧

I bend but do not break.

JEAN DE LA FONTAINE

"How much more can one man take?" the psalmist asks, and it is a question that has been on the lips of many ever since. There are those people to whom suffering and hardship seem to attract like metal to a magnet. For these people (and maybe we would at times count ourselves among their number) there seems to be no escaping the suffering that hovers over and around them. How much can people take?

Although the answer to this question perhaps cannot be stated in a demonstrable way, an answer can be stated nonetheless: God will not allow us to take on more than we can handle. This doesn't always seem like the best answer to us—indeed, it can seem far from it—but when we're bending, it's the only answer there is.

❧ 8 ❧

If we had no winter, the spring would not be so pleasant:
if we did not sometimes taste of adversity,
prosperity would not be so welcome.

ANNE BRADSTREET

It can be a little trite, this notion that we wouldn't be able to fully appreciate the goodness of life without experiencing its loss, and there are probably times—such as in the midst of dark moments—where not many of us would subscribe to it. But there is clearly something here. Those moments in our lives where we suffer—like it or not—do temper us, do change our outlook on life.

How this can be a comfort in the midst of our suffering, however, remains—at least to me anyway—a mystery. But it's a mystery not unworthy of spending my life figuring out. Much like the mystery of the Cross to which it is bound.

❦9❦

A thousand ages in Thy sight
Are like an evening gone.

ISAAC WATTS

Father Theodore is 99 years old and one of the holiest people I know. He never misses prayer; he never seems to get too upset when things around him don't go perfectly; he always has a smile to offer in the corridor. I'm not sure if Father Theodore was this holy as a young man—indeed, no one is, as he has outlived anyone who could tell. But I would have to think that some of his holiness comes from being able to put things in perspective. What seems so absolutely pressing to us now may not seem so pressing with the passage of time, although we have a hard time believing it. But we must believe it, we who profess to honor One who is Lord of all the ages.

❦10❦

Lord save us! We are perishing!

MATTHEW 8:25

Once as a freshman in college, on a weekend trip to Chicago, my friends and I got so lost that we ended up miles and miles into Indiana and didn't even know it. Chicago is a wonderful yet aggravating city, and even though we had a map, the streets there didn't seem to go straight. And if they did go straight they seemed to change names without warning.

Life, especially a life marked by loss, can seem much the same way. We long for a road map to help us know how to get through and around obstacles, only to find that the ways are crooked and just may change on us in the middle of the road. Our only hope, our only map, is Jesus Christ, who travailed the ways of sorrow and suffering Himself and so most certainly knows how to show us where we need to go.

❊ 11 ❊

Zaccheus he
Did climb the tree
Our Lord to see.

THE NEW ENGLAND PRIMER

I frequently say that if a seven-foot-tall woman with a bee-hive hairdo wants to see a movie, not only will she choose the same movie that I am seeing, but will most likely sit in the seat in front of me. Life is filled with obstacles that can get in the way of what our vision truly needs to be. But all too often we get so caught up in the obstacle that we can quit trying to see the things we should.

Not so with Zaccheus. His solution to not being able to see the Lord (who should be the destination of all our hopeful glances) was to climb above anything that would obscure his vision. And he was rewarded for it—as we will be rewarded.

❊ 12 ❊

I cannot reach it, and my striving eye
Dazzles at it, as at eternity.

HENRY VAUGHAN

"Your mother's in Heaven now," I heard more times than I could possibly count. In the weeks following her death, I couldn't quite grasp what that meant because I thought of my mother as I had always known her—a warm, living person of flesh and blood. I was quite unsure what this spirit-world place was supposed to be about. And so all those proclamations of my mother's presence there really did little to comfort me.

But I did feel comfort on my Dad's lap, answering questions that I know had to be painful to hear. I felt comfort as my sister rubbed my feet. I felt comfort in my grandma's arms, calling me her "Baby." And I soon discovered that if I wanted to fully understand the dazzling love of Heaven, I needed only to look around at the dazzling love I felt here, on earth. And it made Heaven all that more accessible.

❧13❧

A man who has nothing can whistle in a robber's face.

JUVENAL

There are those who talk about poverty in terms of people not being able to have their basic needs met and how we go about the business of making sure that more people get what they need and deserve. There are those relatively few in number who talk about poverty as a good thing, that the only way to true happiness comes by way of detachment. Many perhaps would say that this latter notion of poverty is best left to monks and nuns.

I would disagree. Whereas we need to work to eradicate the first kind of poverty, I think too we need to embrace the second kind of poverty, however that may look in the individual circumstances of our lives. Because if we are truly poor then we are in a better mindset to accept what we have been given and recognize when it comes from God.

❧14❧

The time to be happy is now,
The place to be happy is here,
The way to be happy is to make others so.

ROBERT GREEN INGERSOLL

When I was in college, sitting in a particularly boring lecture, I would look at the classroom door and imagine someone coming in and telling me that he was sent here by the Pope and needed me to come with him to Rome because John Paul had a delicate mission that he could entrust only to me. Or he would tell me that he was sent there by Paul McCartney, and the three surviving Beatles had decided that they wanted to get back together and replace John with me. Before long the class would be over and I would scurry out into the hall, clueless as to what we had just been discussing.

The Pope or the Beatles have never called me and now I wonder how much more I could have learned, grown, if I had paid attention to the moment and not wished it away.

❧15❧

Who has seen the wind?
Neither you nor I:
But when the trees bow down their heads,
The wind is passing by.

CHRISTINA GEORGINA ROSSETTI

Once I was talking to a class of second graders. We were supposed to talk about religion, but as is the delightful way of second graders, topics tend to be a bit less constrictive and the planned topic was broadened to include my dog, their dogs, hamsters, pizza and Nintendo.

Eventually, however, I was able to steer things back to religion and the question was asked how we knew there was a God. I tried to talk about faith—just somehow knowing—but wasn't getting through to them. Just then, a kid shouted out that he knew there was a God because his dad took him to see the Cardinals play once and bought him a soda, even though his mother said before they left not to have any soda, that it would keep him up all night. I didn't quite see the connection, but the lad seemed to get knowing nods from his classmates.

❧16❧

I give you a wise and discerning mind;
no one like you has been before you
and no one like you shall arise after you.

I KINGS 3:12

God approached Solomon with an amazing offer: Ask something of me and I will give it to you. Imagine how enormous that offer was. Like Aladdin's famous genie, God was granting absolutely anything. And for what did Solomon wish? Wisdom, an understanding heart.

How much easier life would be if instead of trying to wish away sorrow we would instead seek to understand it—and our God and one another—better.

❧ 17 ❧

And he left them, and getting into the boat again,
he went across to the other side.

MARK 8:13

We are taught: "If at first you don't succeed, try, try again." And this is sage advice for just about any area of life. We must face our struggles with fierce determination, with perseverance. There is grace in the struggle, we know, so we should stick with it.

There is also grace in knowing when we need to step away from the struggle, however. Losing ourselves in a beautiful piece of music, taking a walk, reading a book, seeing a movie can help us put things in perspective and maybe the struggle won't look so monumental from the other shore.

Losing ourselves in a beautiful piece of music,
taking a walk, reading a book, seeing a movie
can help us put things in perspective
and maybe the struggle won't look
as monumental from the other shore.

❧18❧

When a thought takes one's breath away,
a lesson on grammar seems an impertinence.

THOMAS WENTWORTH HIGGINSON

These words were written to introduce the poetry of Emily Dickinson. Dickinson's poetry is wondrous, mad, exhilarating, gut-wrenching and oh-so-alive. People who took too great a pain talking about the oddities of her grammar, meter and punctuation were completely missing the picture of the greatness of her work.

It is a tendency for all of us to concentrate so much on the punctuation and rules of grammar that we miss the breathtaking grandeur of the poem. If we think that we know God and what He wants from us only from concentrating on rigid rules and formulae, then we are not taking into account the life-changing beauty of His Word which—contrary to all rules of grammar—is spoken without any punctuation at all but goes on forever.

❧19❧

Let each man think himself an act of God,
His mind a thought, his life a breath of God.

PHILIP JAMES BAILEY

I was practicing the organ in the church one day when a family came in—a mother, father and a child that looked to be about three years of age. I ceased playing for a while so that they could have a little silence to accompany their discovery of the church. As I watched them, I encountered a marvelous sight: The three year old had discovered that if she made a noise in the church, the noise continued on seconds after she ceased making it. What sheer delight this discovery produced in her, and what embarrassment for her parents as they tried to get her to stop filling the silent church with noise.

What a lovely image. I reflected later on the continuity of the breath of God present in us all. Nothing can silence the Word that His breath produced, and it continues long after it is spoken.

❧ 20 ❧

Pleasant speech multiplies friends,
a gracious tongue multiples courtesies.

SIRACH 6:5

"I vant to be alone," Greta Garbo (or was it Talullah Bankhead?) purred. We all know, at times, what that desire is all about. There are times when the rigors of life have so accumulated that the presence of people in our lives—even family and friends—makes us feel crowded, irritable. And often before we can even think about it we have said harsh or thoughtless words, perhaps desiring to make someone pay for the strife that is whirling inside of us. And harsh and thoughtless words can bring about hurt feelings.

It is no crime to want to be alone every now and then, and it is certainly no crime to purr that to our own loved ones. It's just better to purr than to roar.

❧ 21 ❧

The Israelites went into the sea on dry ground,
the waters forming a wall for them on their right and on their left.

EXODUS 14:22

Not long after I began writing this book, I was in a bookstore and decided to look at what offerings were available on grief and loss. I picked up one book written by a psychologist and in it she spoke of grief using prepositions like "around" and "over." She's the expert, and there is something to be said about the psychological necessity of maneuvering around our grief and getting over our grief. But I'm not sure in the end I agree with her model.

What model would I offer in its stead? The model of the people of Israel, who knew that the only sure way to freedom was to go into the midst of dark waters surrounded by all that could crush them. It's risky, of course, but the outcome is nothing short of the Promised Land.

❧ 22 ❧

We don't see the end of the tunnel, but I must say I don't think
it is darker than it was a year ago, and in some ways lighter.

JOHN FITZGERALD KENNEDY

There are few people of a certain age who can't recall exactly where
they where when they heard the news. The very world was rocked to its
core: A nation had lost a leader; a family had lost a son; and the world
itself seemed to lose some of its light. The unthinkable had happened;
how could we move on? The question has been asked again and again
when other families have lost their children, when the worlds of others
have seen a diminishment in light: How can we move on?

His own words serve as the answer. We go forward, bit by bit, even
though the tunnel around us is dark and indeed may be dark for some
time to come. But perhaps we will slowly come to understand that the
light at the end is getting bigger.

❧ 23 ❧

Then one of them, when he saw that he was healed,
turned back, praising God with a loud voice.
He prostrated himself at Jesus' feet and thanked him.

LUKE 17:15-16

He had to give thanks. One encounter with the man Jesus Christ and
suddenly he was whole, healed, and his life would never be the same.
Before, if he were to reflect on his life, it would be nothing but a vision
of cruel possibilities, each scenario played out in his mind like music
out of tune—grating, cacophonous, disturbing. But that had changed.
Life now played itself out with realities that had never been a part of his
world before: hope, light, life, love. The others with him on his journey
might not agree but he had to give thanks. He knew, ultimately, that
the thanksgiving was an integral part of the cure.

❧ 24 ❧

They ate their food with glad and generous hearts,
praising God and having the goodwill of all the people.

ACTS 2:46-47

They had to give thanks. Gathered in homes and cemeteries our ancestors in the Christian faith recognized that an encounter with Jesus had so changed them that they would never be the same. And so they gathered to give thanks. In a world that was hostile to their message, that could strip them of their very life and dignity just for professing His name, they nevertheless gathered. In rooms around their world they gathered to sing songs, to praise the goodness of their Savior, and to break bread as He commanded them. They had to give thanks. They knew that thanksgiving was an integral part of being nourished.

❧ 25 ❧

I give you thanks, O Lord, with my whole heart.

PSALM 137

Even in our darkest moments I think we need to know how important it is to give thanks. We are aware that our encounters with Jesus can so change us that we—even in the midst of a world that can still be hostile to His message—know hope, light, life, love. The blessings of this world are mere reflections of those encounters and we must always strive to mirror the praise of that leper, of those early Christians, of all who have been touched by His presence, by his love. And so we too must give thanks. We know ultimately that giving thanks is an integral part of living.

❧ 26 ❧

*My marks and scars I carry with me, to be a witness for me,
that I have fought His battles who now will be my rewarder.*

JOHN BUNYAN

My first trip to the beach—one of my favorite places on earth—after my last two major surgeries filled me with great dread. In order to bask in the warmth of the sun I would have to expose my rather significant scars for all the world to see. I saw them as ugly, these scars, and wanted to hide them. But the lure of the sun was too great for me to ignore and so to the beach I went.

I was walking along self-consciously when an older gentleman approached me, pointed to my stomach and exclaimed, "That's quite a scar you have there, buddy!" He then unbuttoned his own shirt, showed me a scar of his own and said, "They're beautiful, aren't they? It shows we've survived."

He was right, of course, about those scars, and about the ones that aren't so readily visible.

❧ 27 ❧

If one blind person guides another, both will fall into a pit.

MATTHEW 15:14

There are as many ways to deal with grief and loss as there are people in the world. Books and pamphlets have been written, seminars given, sermons preached that help people who are awash in grief to somehow make sense of it all. And it is a good thing there are so many because different people need different things.

Not all the ways are good ways. People who try to escape their grief through sedating it are ultimately not helping themselves. Nor are people who ignore their grief and act like it doesn't exist. And so whereas many who have gone this road before us can serve as our guides, many cannot, for nothing comes of the blind leading the blind except for darkness.

❧28❧

He endowed them with strength like his own…
and gave them dominion over beasts and birds.

SIRACH 17:3

Bosnia; Croatia; Rwanda; Chechnya. The list goes on and on of places where people have suffered debilitating tragedies, where famine and violence and death and suffering seem to go hand in hand with the very names of the places themselves, as if you can't really say any of the places without onerous adjectives hovering nearby.

But even if the names, now so familiar, are of pieces of land far away, the names are essentially of people—people exactly like you and me, who have the same vision and hope that we have. People who cry out to make sense of it all. People who—perhaps most amazingly—survive it all: the degradation, the strife, the utter desolation. And in the midst of it all, in the midst of the suffering, is a God who has given them strength. And that strength is ours as well.

❧29❧

God's mill grinds slow, but sure.

GEORGE HERBERT

We'll feel better some day, we're told, God will see to it. And then we look around the world and see all kinds of people starving whom God is supposed to be caring for; we see people shackled in darkness, longing for but not receiving the light of mercy. We see these things and we wonder: If God is tending to these people why isn't more being done? It doesn't bode well for those of us who are weighted down by our own sorrows.

It is faith, pure and simple, that allows us to see that God is tending to these people. He is there in the suffering, He is there among the poverty, He is there with the captives longing to be free, He is there in our sorrow. We may not approve of His timeline, but faith tells us that what He wills, and not our own will, is of the ultimate importance. And so we wait and hope as God's mill grinds on.

❦ 30 ❦

Then the disciples came and asked him,
"Why do you speak to them in parables?"
MATTHEW 13:10

I'm not sure, as a young boy, if I would have understood what it really meant to be a part of a family that extended beyond my own if it weren't for my Gramps, and the stories he told of his days growing up, of his parents and brothers and sisters who—I realized—were my great-grandparents and great-aunts and uncles. I am not sure I would have felt a connection to my father's youth had he not told me stories of his days on the farm. As a boy, I figured out who I was and where I came from through listening to the stories of those around me.

If we are having difficulty understanding loss in our lives, perhaps we can turn to the story of the man Jesus and find in Him not only insights into suffering and loss, but learn who we are and where we came from.

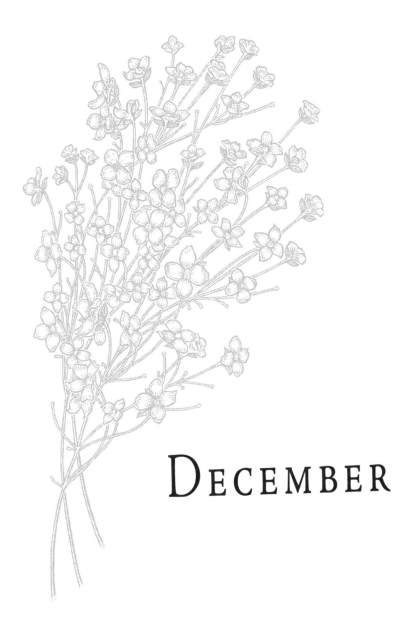

DECEMBER

❧ 1 ❧

Every generous act of giving, with every perfect gift, is from above,
coming down from the Father of lights,
with whom there is no variation or shadow due to change.

JAMES 1:17

Before my mother died, at Christmastime we presented her with a
mother's ring with one stone each for her three children. As she opened
the small box she was overcome with emotion and began weeping
intensely. I was just a small boy and I didn't understand how getting
a gift—one that she obviously liked—could bring about tears that
usually were reserved for bad things like pain and frustration. Maybe
it wasn't such a good gift after all, I thought.

I know now, in a way I could never have known then, that gifts are
about more than just feeling good. Gifts are about offering a part of who
we are—complete with pain—to those whom we love. Viewed in this
light, even her very tears ended up being a gift.

❧ 2 ❧

In this you rejoice.

1 PETER 1:6

What an amazing statement of faith this is. Peter is writing of trials
and sufferings that his flock may have to endure, of death and fear and
confusion. And he is telling them even in the midst of death and fear
and confusion, they have cause for rejoicing. It seems a little optimistic
at best and downright crazy at worst. But Peter obviously believes it
and expects his flock to believe it as well, regardless of the cost.

And so this proclamation is given to us as well. And we are expected
to believe it regardless of the cost. Optimistic? Most definitely. Crazy?
Perhaps. But we've most likely rejoiced over crazier things than this.

❦ 3 ❦

We pardon to the extent that we love.
FRANÇOIS, DUC DE ROCHEFOUCAULD

I had to face it eventually, the anger I felt toward my mother. It would crop up on days like the Friday before Mother's Day when my gradeschool classmates would be busy making something beautiful for their mothers and I had to do something for my father or sister instead. It would crop up on those first few birthdays when hers was not among the faces sitting around the table. And every time it would crop up I would tell myself that it was wrong to be angry with her—it wasn't her fault that she died—but the anger was there nonetheless.

But deep within myself I have had to learn not to be angry with myself and not to be angry with her: Both of us have done what we could. And this release, this pardon, comes from nothing less than the love we shared and continue to share in some way.

❦ 4 ❦

Moses said to the people:
"Has anything so great as this ever happened?"
DEUTERONOMY 4:32

Every now and then we need to hear it whether we want to or not. Every now and then we need to sit down and make ourselves realize just what amazing things God has done in this world, even if we are having a hard time seeing it now. Because the fact remains that indeed nothing so great ever did happen before. God sent His Son into the world to lead captive souls into freedom, and because of His death and resurrection we know that those whom we love and who have gone before have union with Him in a way that the people of Moses' day did not. We need to hear it.

❧ 5 ❧

Come to me, all you that are weary
and are carrying heavy burdens, and I will give you rest.

MATTHEW 11:28

I was never supposed to drink straight out of the bottle, but I always did. In the refrigerator, as soon as you opened the door, was an old orange juice bottle that we kept filled with water. On summer days after having been hard at the work of play, I could hardly wait to rush into the coolness of the kitchen, feel the icy blast of air as I opened the refrigerator door and reach for the bottle. Who had time to go to the cabinet, get a glass, pour the water in the glass, and politely return the bottle to the refrigerator? Certainly not I, who relished the cool refreshment even as it spilled over my quaking chin and collected in a puddle on the floor.

Jesus desires to refresh us so. Let us never forget this even in the midst of the heat.

❧ 6 ❧

For with God all things are possible.

MARK 10:27

We don't always believe it, this business of all things being possible with God. We can recount all the wonders God has done in the past; we can get all misty-eyed as lisping third-grade angels announce the birth of the Messiah while antsy shepherds with towels on their heads shift nervously nearby; we can wax eloquently about that empty tomb with the sun rising behind it and the Hallelujah Chorus ringing out its glorious polyphony.

But all that is in the past. What about now? What about the possibility of God taking what hurts within us and making it whole? What about the possibility that, not only can God heal us, He can take that which has made us hurt in the first place and make it an instrument of our healing? How bizarre. But how entirely possible with this great God of the impossible.

❧ 7 ❧

Because God's gifts put man's best dreams to shame.

ELIZABETH BARRETT BROWNING

Who would have dreamed of a world filled with light and darkness, land and water, fish and fowl, men and women? God would have, that's who. He who said: "Let there be light." Who would have dreamed of a virgin giving birth to a child? God would, that's who. He who received Mary's word: "Let it be done unto me according to your word." Who would have dreamed of a man broken, beaten and killed rising from the dead? God would, that's who. He who inspired the words: "He has risen, as He said He would."

And the list is endless, the amazing gifts that God has bestowed and continues to bestow upon us, His awe-filled people. And the point needs to be acknowledged over and over again: Let us never assume that just because we can't imagine something, God cannot; for His dreams continue to make life happen.

❧ 8 ❧

The kingdom of heaven is like a treasure buried in a field.

MATTHEW 13:44

I recently received an e-mail from a friend who I hadn't spoken to in years. We hadn't had any kind of a falling out, it's just that time and distance took its toll and we lost touch. Then quite unexpectedly I heard from him, and it was a wonderful surprise, a treasured discovery.

Life can be filled with such surprises if we keep our eyes open for them. And finding these treasures can help make sure that moments of sorrow never completely bury moments of joy.

❦9❦

Return, O faithless children, says the Lord.

JEREMIAH 3:14

Once when my brother and I were roughhousing, he accidentally put his foot through an aquarium, causing slimy water and fish to cascade over the floor. Aware that our father was going to hit the roof, and having seen too many Saturday matinees on Channel 11 where the falsely-accused man is given shelter by an understanding friar, we hopped on our bikes and rode to the church, allowing the quiet of its space to quiet our own fractured breathing. Eventually, however, we knew we would have to return home to face the music.

It can be our first response to escape those things in our lives that cause us discomfort, pain or fear. And escape for a while can provide a necessary respite, a quiet place to think. But escape is not a solution. Reluctantly we need to face the music, even if it sounds like a dirge.

❦10❦

Long is the way
And hard, that out of hell leads up to light.

JOHN MILTON

I live on a hill, a fact which is quite enjoyable when I am going out for a bicycle ride but lamentable upon my return. Legs burning, breath heaving, I make my ascent, willing myself not to get off my bike and walk it. "I can do this," I tell myself, regardless of the fact that I am out of shape, that my legs burn, and it feels as if my chest is about to explode. And when I arrive at the top I don't have any enormous feeling of accomplishment; I don't prance around like Rocky while stirring music swirls around me. No—when you live on a hill you have to expect that there are going to be all kinds of uphill climbs and just be about the business of getting up there.

Life is no different.

❧ 11 ❧

Are you not from of old, O Lord my God, my Holy One?

HABAKKUK 1:12

Time can be as varied as the circumstances in which it presents itself. Sitting in a dentist's chair, mouth agape and filled with tools, a few minutes can seem to last much longer. The same time can seem to rush by if we are spending it eating our favorite dessert, feeling the taste of the last bite slowly dissipate from our mouths. Time, it seems, is relative.

Which is a good insight when pondering the nature of sorrow and suffering in our lives. God is eternal, and though it seems like we can at times suffer for an eternity we know that it is but an instant in God's eyes. And the only way to make that instant more bearable for us whose perception of time can be sometimes languorous, sometimes swift, is to make it our constant prayer that we may see more and more as God sees.

❧ 12 ❧

The soul's dark cottage, batter'd and decay'd,
Lets in new light through chinks that Time has made.

EDMUND WALLER

While I was preaching a parish mission, a woman came up to me and said that young as I was, it was obvious I possessed an old soul. At the time I wasn't sure if the appropriate response was "Thank you" or "I do not!" The more I thought about it, however, the more I decided it was a compliment. I would like to think that the things that have happened in my life—good and bad—have perhaps wizened my soul beyond my years. I am comforted by the thought that though I may be young or immature or downright goofy, there is a part of me that is beyond all that.

The same can probably be said for many of us. The experiences of our lives have affected us in the depths of our souls in ways that we may not realize. The only way to make sense of it all is to be open to that Light which comes from above to illumine us with insight.

❧13❧

Concerning this salvation,
the prophets made careful search and inquiry.

1 PETER 1:10

They left no stone unturned, those prophets of old. God told them to speak and as their mouths opened to utter His marvelous poetry they themselves looked for clues to the nature of life and love in the very words that came out. They wondered what God had in store for them, what amazing and terrible things would come to pass for those whom He had chosen. And the clues to it all were on their own lips as they spoke of wonders they themselves could only begin to imagine.

What they only could imagine, we now know. Because what was promised by the prophets so long ago has been fulfilled. And if we want to know what God has in store for us, what amazing and terrible things will come to pass for us, we must listen to their words and listen to the ultimate Word, Jesus Christ. We need search and examine no further.

❧14❧

Do not appear before the Lord empty-handed,
for all that you offer is in fulfillment of the commandment.

SIRACH 35:6-7

"Offer it up" used to be a phrase that sprung from the lips of Catholics whenever they had to endure something unattractive, ranging from something as enormous as one of life's major tragedies to something as ordinary as a trip to the dentist. The notion is that when we must endure something that we would rather not, we can link our pain to the pain of the Cross and so make it a prayer to God.

Some would say this is old-fashioned, but I would disagree. If we believe that everything that happens to us in life can in the end be some mysterious gift from God, then it goes to follow that when we receive one of these gifts—especially when we can't quite see the nature of the gift—we need to offer it back to God. It is only through this offering that we can begin to see how varied God's gifts are.

❦ 15 ❦

There was a man sent from God whose name was John.
He came as a witness to testify to the light,
so that all might believe through him.
He himself was not the light, but he came to testify to the light.

JOHN 1:6-8

How exciting he must have been, John the Baptist. Clad in camel's hair and leather, munching away on grasshoppers, he must have made quite a sight—a figure that, like Errol Flynn, might make women swoon and men want to be like him. I imagine his voice had to be thunderous and deep and perhaps set him apart more than anything else. It was that voice that the prophet Isaiah had foretold of thousands of years before that made people look at their world and its possibilities a bit differently—to imagine a world where the lowly receive glad tidings, the brokenhearted are healed, and captives receive liberty. It was that voice that made people sit up and take note that their world was about to change forever. It was that voice that, if we listen to it, can still call us to imagine our world differently and even heal our broken hearts.

*It was that voice that, if we listen to it,
can still call us to imagine our world differently
and even heal our broken hearts.*

❧16❧

To all who received him, who believed in his name,
he gave power to become children of God.

JOHN 1:12

There are those who would say that it is unfortunate that we don't have in our world today a figure like John the Baptist. There are those who would say that above the clamor and din of this world, no voice rises to show us the way as he did so many years ago. I don't believe that. Because you see, the same Lord whom John foretold will come again. This has been promised to us, this we believe. And just as John's voice rang out with the possibilities of accepting an encounter with the one who is to save us, just as John's voice rang out with notions of what we can do to prepare for that coming, so too I believe there are voices in our world today calling out the same ideas. We need only listen to these voices wherever we may encounter them.

❧17❧

I will put my law within them,
and I will write it on their hearts.

JEREMIAH 31:33

For months after the death of my mother I would cry myself to sleep and wonder when I would feel better. I overheard someone say in reference to me, "His poor little heart is broken," and I figured that's what was wrong. How then could I fix it? What could mend my heart? The answers didn't seem to be coming.

In retrospect, however, I realize that every time someone around me reached out to me, every time someone voiced their love, every time I was allowed to feel—if only for a moment—that things were good in the world, my heart was healing, gently caressed by a God for whom all those people were instruments. I know now what a solace it can be to recognize that caring touch when it's happening.

❧18❧

That many people read a song
Who will not read a sermon.

WINTHROP MACKWORTH PRAED

My friend David teases me about finding some of the answers to life's basic questions in the lines of pop songs, and I have to admit that it is something I tend to do—shallow as that may seem. I'm convinced that people who are inspired to write truly good music and lyrics are inspired by the same Spirit who hopefully helps me on my sermons. Whereas I may find Biblical allusions to help get across the notion of love, does it not get across the same point when Peter Gabriel says that in someone's eyes he sees "the doorway to a thousand churches?"

And so if there is a song that seems to give voice to our grief, seems to speak to where we truly are, it's not necessarily shallow. It could just be the Spirit.

❧19❧

I will now call to mind the works of the Lord,
and will declare what I have seen.

SIRACH 42:15

People who don't live in Chicago always seem to want to go to Rush Street when they are visiting. The area is filled with people and—as is often the case with areas filled with people—activity that could best be described as perhaps not the moral ideal. And because of this, there are frequently street preachers perched on corners, yelling at people to reform their lives or else. Say what you will about their message, one has to respect their desire to yell the Gospel message (or at least their take on it) to anyone who will listen.

There is something to be said about sharing our faith with others. Even if the faith we share is one filled with confusion, proclaiming it helps us understand it better and can certainly help others.

❦20❦

Many sternly ordered him to be quiet,
be he cried out all the louder.

MARK 10:48

There are times when our souls are filled with joy and we wish to shout the wonders of creation to the world. There are times when we are hurt and we wish to shout our pain to the world. There are times when we are perplexed and we want to shout our search for the answers to the world. There are times when we feel alone and we want to shout our need for others to the world.

And there are times when the world doesn't want to hear what we have to shout at it. It is at these times we need to shout all the louder.

❦21❦

O brave new world,
That has such people in't!

WILLIAM SHAKESPEARE

Father Godfrey, one of my oldest, dearest friends, is quite a piece of work. Hilarious and serious, pious and irreverent, aggravating and soothing, loquacious and listening, he has the ability to allow me to weep my sorrows without ever letting the weeping have the final word, silencing it with the louder boisterousness of laughter.

People in our lives like Godfrey can't take sorrow away but they can take a world clouded in mist and make it seem less dark somehow. They can serve as models to us that although we may weep, joy is all around us, ready to burst through into our lives and into our world at any moment. And what a great world it can be when we allow those who love us to help shape it.

❦ 22 ❦

Abraham was the father of Jacob,
and Jacob the father of Judah and his brothers...

MATTHEW 1:2

Abraham knew it, an emptiness. Called by God to be the father of a people, there was still something missing, still some distance between him and this mysterious God. And so when God told him to sacrifice his own son, he agreed; maybe in hopes that this horrible ultimate act of love would fill the emptiness that must have been a part of him. God, we know, didn't allow him to carry through with it, but Abraham was willing, so strong was this emptiness. In the midst of it all—the searching, the longing, the confusion, the doubt—Abraham knew that only God could fill the emptiness. He needed only wait for it to happen.

❦ 23 ❦

...And Salmon the father of Boaz by Rahab,
and Boaz the father of Obed by Ruth...

MATTHEW 1:5

Ruth knew this emptiness. Widowed and among a foreign people, she could have gone back to her own land, her own people. But she stayed with her mother-in-law, singing sweetly, "Wherever you go I will go, wherever you live I will live." These words of love filled the emptiness that had to have been there. In the midst of it all—the searching, the longing, the confusion, the doubt—Ruth knew that only God could fill the emptiness. She needed only wait for it to happen.

❧24❧

...And Obed the father of Jesse,
and Jesse the father of King David.

MATTHEW 1:6

King David knew this emptiness. Chosen as a youth to be Israel's king, bonded in a special covenant with God, he still longed to know Him better, to be closer to Him, singing, "To you, O Lord, I call; my rock, do not refuse to hear me, for if you are silent to me, I shall be like those who go down to the pit" (Psalm 28). David wrote many such psalms, but the emptiness remained. In the midst of it all—the searching, the longing, the confusion, the doubt—David knew that only God could fill the emptiness. He needed only wait for it to happen.

❧25❧

...And Jacob the father of Joseph the husband of Mary,
of whom Jesus was born, who is called the Messiah.

MATTHEW 1:16

We have a lot in common with people like Abraham, Ruth, David, our ancestors. We too glimpse emptiness in our lives from time to time. But it is only a glimpse. If our ancestors knew the emptiness of questioning whether God was always present, we know the reality of One who was born into our very midst. If our ancestors knew the emptiness of questioning whether God really knew their pain, we know the reality of One like us, subject to suffering, not immune to our struggles. And if our ancestors knew the emptiness of questioning whether God loved them, we know the reality of One who loved us so much that He willingly died for our sake and left in His wake an empty tomb to mock the emptiness that had once been present. Our emptiness can be filled. We need wait no longer.

✵26✵

Now to him who is able to keep you from falling,
and to make you stand without blemish in the presence of his glory
with rejoicing...

JUDE 1:24

Some people turn to material objects, thinking that possessions alone can make life more worthwhile. Some turn to events, as if merely keeping busy will quell any hunger that may be within them. Some turn to wrongdoing, as if doing something they know is wrong will help them feel right, if only for a moment. Whatever the case, the fact remains that all of us turn to all kinds of things to fill that which is empty inside of us, to make us forget loneliness, grief, sorrow.

The author of the letter of Jude perhaps understood the human nature that makes us chase after so much to try and make ourselves feel better. But he also knew the truth: All of it is in vain, for there is only One who can be all things for all people, quelling hungers, easing sorrow, inspiring exultation and glory.

✵27

The attempt and not the deed confounds us.

WILLIAM SHAKESPEARE

Many have said that the hardest part of the particular style of praying with the Scriptures known as *lectio divina* (holy reading) is not the contemplation on the text, or the meditation, or even putting to words what we have gained from the experience, but just opening the Bible. Once the beginning is attempted the rest usually flows a little easier.

So it is with the work of grief. There may be all kinds of things that we tell ourselves we need to do, all kinds of hurdles that we know await us, but just setting our minds to the task and doing something is usually the hardest part. We need to be confident that, just as when we open the Bible we know that God can speak to us, so too does He gently encourage us to do what we must do if we only open our minds to the beginning of the task.

❧28❧

I will greatly rejoice in the Lord, my whole being shall exult.
For he has clothed me with the garments of salvation
and he has covered me with the robe of righteousness.

ISAIAH 61:10

My mother had a blue velveteen robe with some sort of gold orphery on it that she frequently wore. I remember thinking as a child that it was a magnificent piece of clothing, and that she was like a beautiful queen when she wore it, regal and filled with strength. As I grew to adulthood, it was disappointing to look at photographs in which my mother wore the robe because I could see that it was an ordinary robe and that she was often frail and sickly in it.

Our memories of our loved ones can be clothed in all kinds of idealistic accoutrements, and it can be sad for us to acknowledge that things were not always necessarily as we perceived them. But the love that covers our memories and the love with which God can clothe them now can indeed bring about rejoicing.

❧29❧

You explain nothing, O poet,
but thanks to you all things become explicable.

PAUL CLAUDEL

I gave the address at a cancer survivor's day, and afterwards had the opportunity to discuss the disease with my fellow survivors. I was amazed at the amount of metaphor flying around the room like an excited bird: "I felt like a piece of luggage left at the airport that everyone kept looking into and putting back on the conveyor." "I felt like I had been invaded by an army with nothing to defend me." "I feel like I am constantly being followed by a thief, never knowing when he's going to mug me."

We may think that there is no one who feels the way we do, and to an extent we're right. But writers, poets, musicians and painters have tried to express at least some of the human condition, and they just might have an idea of what we're experiencing if we listen to them.

❧30❧

"Pass in, pass in," the angels say,
"In to the upper doors,
Nor count compartments of the floors,
But mount to paradise
By the stairway of surprise."

RALPH WALDO EMERSON

There are people who read the last page of the book first, and I have to be honest that these people annoy me. It seems to me that part of the wonder of life is the finding out of things, and if we know the answer before the question gets asked then we're missing out on a great deal of where that question may take us. The unknown element of surprise can be a risky venture, but there is clearly a pay-off in risking a surprise.

Definitely something to be remembered when we think we know all the answers or can find them out. Our only real avenue of discovery lies in the surprise of God's love for us, and just where that may lead us is a mystery indeed.

Our only real avenue of discovery lies
in the surprise of God's love for us.

Additional Grief Resources

THE DEATH OF A PARENT
Reflections for Adults Mourning the Loss of a Father or Mother
DELLE CHATMAN

This book is filled with stories of people who have lost a parent and how they worked through their grief. A spiritual reflection concludes each of the sections.   128 pages, paperback, $9.95

THE DEATH OF A WIFE
Reflections for a Grieving Husband
ROBERT L. VOGT

A collection of poignant reflections for any husband mourning the death of his wife. Each of the thirty-one brief stories, remembrances, meditations and poems considers a different facet of the grieving process for men.

112 pages, $9.95

THE DEATH OF A HUSBAND
Reflections for a Grieving Wife
HELEN REICHERT LAMBIN

Over forty reflections for any wife mourning the death of her husband offer insights that will touch a woman's heart, heal her soul, and point out new and hopeful directions for her life.   128 pages, $9.95

THE DEATH OF A CHILD
Reflections for Grieving Parents
ELAINE E. STILLWELL

Filled with examples of people who have lost a child and how they dealt with the reality of that event. This collection of life-giving lessons touches on the wide range of emotions and situations that parents encounter after the death of their child.   160 pages, $9.95

THE NEW DAY JOURNAL
A Journey from Grief to Healing
MAURYEEN O'BRIEN

Designed to help those mourning the loss of a loved one work their way through the four tasks of grief: accepting the reality of the loss, experiencing the pain of grief, adjusting to change, and creating memories and goals.

96 pages, $9.95

Available from booksellers or call (800) 397-2282
www.actapublications.com

❧ 31 ❧

I am the Alpha and the Omega, the first and the last,
the beginning and the end!

REVELATION 22:13

For each ending there is a beginning—the inescapable consequence
of time. But to say this so easily is to not put proper emphasis on the
toll it takes on us, we who have to endure relinquishing the comfort of
endings and step forth into the unfamiliarity of new beginnings. It is
far from easy, this business of ending and beginning.

And the only way to endure is to never lose sight of the One who is
the beginning and end of all there is.

Let us renew ourselves to begin again in Him.